DATE DUE

JUL 0 5			
JUL 2 1			
DEC 0 4			
APR 1			

Demco, Inc. 38-293

**Public Policy,
Science, and
Environmental Risk**

Brookings Dialogues on Public Policy

The presentations and discussions at Brookings conferences and seminars often deserve wide circulation as contributions to public understanding of issues of national importance. The Brookings Dialogues on Public Policy series is intended to make such statements and commentary available to a broad and general audience, usually in summary form. The series supplements the Institution's research publications by reflecting the contrasting, often lively, and sometimes conflicting views of elected and appointed government officials, other leaders in public and private life, and scholars. In keeping with their origin and purpose, the Dialogues are not subjected to the formal review procedures established for the Institution's research publications. Brookings publishes them in the belief that they are worthy of public consideration but does not assume responsibility for their accuracy or objectivity. And, as in all Brookings publications, the judgments, conclusions, and recommendations presented in the Dialogues should not be ascribed to the trustees, officers, or other staff members of the Brookings Institution.

Public Policy, Science, and Environmental Risk

Addresses by J. RICHARD CROUT

THOMAS H. MOSS

DENIS PRAGER

MORTON CORN

ROBERT J. MOOLENAAR

GILBERT S. OMENN

JOHN HIGGINSON

WILLIAM W. LOWRANCE

JOHN H. GIBBONS

MONTE C. THRODAHL

presented at a workshop
at the Brookings Institution
on February 28, 1983

Edited by SANDRA PANEM

THE BROOKINGS INSTITUTION
Washington, D.C.

About Brookings

THE BROOKINGS INSTITUTION is a private nonprofit organization devoted to research, education, and publication in economics, government, foreign policy, and the social sciences generally. Its principal purpose is to bring knowledge to bear on the current and emerging public policy problems facing the American people. In its research, Brookings functions as an independent analyst and critic, committed to publishing its findings for the information of the public. In its conferences and other activities, it serves as a bridge between scholarship and public policy, bringing new knowledge to the attention of decisionmakers and affording scholars a better insight into policy issues. Its activities are carried out through three research programs (Economic Studies, Governmental Studies, Foreign Policy Studies), an Advanced Study Program, a Publications Program, and a Social Science Computation Center.

The Institution was incorporated in 1927 to merge the Institute for Government Research, founded in 1916 as the first private organization devoted to public policy issues at the national level; the Institute of Economics, established in 1922 to study economic problems; and the Robert Brookings Graduate School of Economics and Government, organized in 1924 as a pioneering experiment in training for public service. The consolidated institution was named in honor of Robert Somers Brookings (1850–1932), a St. Louis businessman whose leadership shaped the earlier organization.

Brookings is financed largely by endowment and by the support of philanthropic foundations, corporations, and private individuals. Its funds are devoted to carrying out its own research and educational activities. It also undertakes some unclassified government contract studies, reserving the right to publish its findings.

A Board of Trustees is responsible for general supervision of the Institution, approval of fields of investigation, and safeguarding the independence of the Institution's work. The President is the chief administrative officer, responsible for formulating and coordinating policies, recommending projects, approving publications, and selecting the staff.

Contents

Acknowledgments

The workshop whose proceedings follow was a lively and stimulating occasion because of the efforts of many people. I am particularly grateful to Bruce L. R. Smith of the Brookings Institution and Edwin L. Behrens of the American Industrial Health Council for their generous advice in planning the workshop, and to Maxine R. Mennen of the Brookings Advanced Study Program, who supervised the organizational arrangements. Donna J. Roginski prepared the manuscript for publication, and Nancy Snyder did the proofreading.

The Brookings Institution is grateful to the American Industrial Health Council for providing funds to help support the workshop and the publication of this report.

SANDRA PANEM

Washington, D.C.
October 1983

Introduction

SANDRA PANEM

A RECENT CARTOON in the *Chicago Tribune* showed a man and woman watching the evening news on television. The woman asks, "Why should I be worried about fish contaminated with dioxin; won't the acid rain kill them?" The cartoon typifies the renewed public attention to the environment triggered by recent controversies over dioxin, toxic and nuclear waste disposal, and acid rain, and the scandals surrounding the Environmental Protection Agency (EPA) and its handling of enforcement issues.

The history of environmental regulation in the United States abounds with examples of legislative and administrative changes occurring in response to crises. In response to deaths related to poorly manufactured drugs the Food and Drug Administration (FDA) was established in 1938. Similarly, the 1962 publication of Rachel Carson's *Silent Spring* focused public attention on environmental issues, which in turn led to legislation on water and air quality standards. Highly publicized stories about oil tanker breakups in Puerto Rico in 1967 and 1968 and oil-well leakage off the shore of Santa Barbara, California, in 1969 further heightened public concern for the environment. The establishment of the EPA in April 1970 can be viewed as the logical result of rising political pressure for a coordinated federal policy on regulating the quality of the environment.[1] The political importance of environmental issues was shown by Richard Nixon's treatment of these issues in his 1970 State of the Union address: "The great question of the seventies is, shall we surrender to our surroundings, or shall we make our peace with nature and begin to make reparations for the damage we have done to our air, our land and our water?"[2]

The legacy of public sensitivity toward environmental issues remains today. Yet the content of the environmental debate has

1. For a detailed chronological description of these events, see J. Clarence Davies and Barbara S. Davies, *The Politics of Pollution* (Indianapolis, Indiana: Pegasus, Bobbs-Merrill, 1975).

2. Quoted in ibid., p. 9.

I

shifted as we have become more sophisticated about measuring pollution and its consequences. Our ability to detect and measure pollutants in the environment has greatly improved, although not all technical difficulties have been overcome. With improved measurement the need to determine the relative risks of pollutants in different environmental contexts becomes paramount. In the context of the recession of the early 1980s and the Reagan administration's commitment to economic deregulation and more "reasonable" assessment of risks in health and safety regulations, the uncertainties involved in measuring the extent and effects of pollutants have moved into the center of the environmental debate. A June 1982 report from the Conservation Foundation sums up the issue:

> Scientific ignorance or uncertainty characterizes most environmental problems. We do not know much about how to predict the transport of pollutants in air or water, we do not have good ways of measuring or predicting the amount of soil erosion from a field, we do not know the habitat requirements of many endangered species, we have only rudimentary knowledge of how heat circulates inside buildings. The gaps in scientific knowledge are most severe with respect to toxic substances. Many potentially toxic chemicals have not been tested at all, many more have not been tested adequately, and, even for those that have been subjected to the most extensive tests, we are often unsure what the tests mean for human health.
>
> Our monitoring of environmental problems is even more deficient than our scientific knowledge. We have no monitoring data sufficient to describe accurately the extent or developing seriousness of any environmental problem.[3]

The recent study of risk assessment by the National Research Council (NRC) of the National Academy of Sciences was even more emphatic in linking current policy conflicts with improvements in technical measurement capabilities:

> Many decisions of federal agencies in regulating chronic health hazards have been bitterly controversial. The roots of the controversy lie in improvements in scientific and technologic capability to detect potentially hazardous chemicals, in changes in public expectations and concerns about health protection, and in the fact that the costs and benefits of regulatory policies fall unequally.[4]

---

3. Conservation Foundation, *State of the Environment, 1982* (Washington, D.C.: Conservation Foundation, 1982), pp. 6–7.
4. National Research Council, Committee on the Institutional Means for Assessment of Risks to Public Health, *Risk Assessment in the Federal Government: Managing the Process* (Washington, D.C.: National Academy Press, 1983).

The policy challenge now is how to best formulate public policy using new but still inexact and incomplete scientific information.

This volume in the Brookings Dialogues on Public Policy series reports the results of a February 28, 1983, workshop held with support from the American Industrial Health Council to explore the complex issues involved in scientific measurement of environmental risk. The purposes were to articulate the policy issues that concern the use of scientific data in environmental risk assessment and to contribute to the dialogue from which better policy might emerge. The book presents the viewpoints of workshop participants from several sectors—the executive and legislative branches of government, industry, academia, and the policy analysis community.

Areas of consensus

There were several broad areas of consensus among workshop participants. Perhaps the most fundamental point of agreement was that federal regulations are needed, especially in regulating chemical substances that affect human health. A stable and sensible framework is vastly preferable to a constantly changing regulatory regime. The costs of health care attest to the need for the regulation of environmental health hazards: 9.8 percent of the U.S. gross national product was expended in health-related areas in 1981.[5]

Another point of consensus was that the time required for public policy decisions and the time required for generating appropriate scientific information are rarely the same. No permanent solution for this problem is likely to be found, as crises sometimes compel action against a background of inadequate information. In the middle 1970s, for example, a health emergency arose in the shape of a threatened influenza epidemic. The influenza virus was thought to be the same type that had caused severe health and economic problems in 1918. A public health decision was required on whether to mandate a national vaccination program against this "swine flu." For technical reasons the decision had to be made before it was definitively known if the epidemic would really occur.[6] The fiasco that resulted is well known.

5. The figure of 9.8 percent of gross national product includes expenditures for health services and supplies, program administration, insurance, and government and public health activities, as well as research and construction of medical facilities. Robert M. Gibson and Daniel R. Waldo, "National Health Expenditures, 1981," *Health Care Financing Review*, vol. 4 (September 1982), pp. 1–35.

6. Arthur M. Silverstein, *Pure Politics and Impure Science: The Swine Flu Affair* (Johns Hopkins University Press, 1981); and Richard E. Neustadt and Harvey V. Fineberg, *The Swine Flu Affair: Decision-Making on a Slippery Disease* (Department of Health, Education, and Welfare, 1978).

A complementary example of how policy must often be made against a background of incomplete technical data concerns the measurement of chemicals. Our ability to measure minute quantities of some chemical pollutants in the atmosphere is now greater than our knowledge about the effects of these chemicals at low concentrations. Yet clean air legislation requires the establishment of guidelines for specific chemical air pollutants.

In both these cases the scientific information was inadequate, and the ultimate policy decision had to accommodate additional, nonquantitative factors—including "the pressure to act responsibly now." The workshop participants recognized this and agreed that policymakers and scientists should attempt to understand the unique pressures arising from their distinctive missions and backgrounds. To the extent that decisions can be taken out of the crisis framework, and dialogue can replace adversarial roles, the public interest will be better served. The workshop participants agreed that risk assessment is not an exact science and that regulation cannot be absolute. Risk must be balanced against cost and benefits. The "absolute" regulatory stance, exemplified by the Delaney clause of the Food, Drug, and Cosmetic Act, is outdated.

Finally, a most important point of consensus concerned the current adversarial climate in which environmental policy is made. Participants agreed that there is rarely an effective dialogue between industry and government before issues become critical and debate assumes a confrontational character. Under these conditions the possibility of agreement without protracted litigation all but disappears. The recognition that adversarial positions impede effective environmental regulation led to a discussion of how to eliminate the problem. On this point, however, there was little consensus.

Current environmental policy challenges

How can the adversarial atmosphere in which environmental risks are evaluated and regulated be altered so that expertise and divergent opinions are brought into the policymaking process at an early stage? The development of standards and strategies to control environmental risk is a multifaceted problem whose solution requires consideration of inexact and incomplete scientific findings as well as nonscientific information. The current atmosphere fosters the championing of hardline positions rather than the gradual development of consensus. One conclusion from the workshop was that more research must be done to improve both the hard science base on which regulators rely as well as the social science framework used for risk-benefit analysis in regulatory decisionmaking.

How should science experts participate in the policymaking process? Opinions at the workshop ranged from the complete separation of science advice and policy decisions to the opposite extreme where regulations are directly tied to the scientist's quantitative measurements.

Lively discussion was directed to the recommendations of the March 1983 NRC report on risk assessment, which Frank Press, chairman of the National Research Council, transmitted to the commissioner of the Food and Drug Administration. This report had three main objectives: to assess the need to separate administrative risk assessment from risk management; to determine whether all federal risk assessment should be centralized; and to determine whether uniform guidelines for risk assessment should be adopted for all regulatory agencies.

The NRC report recognized the importance of conceptually separating risk assessment from risk management. It also noted that discontent with environmental regulation often focuses on administrative change because of frustration with the inexact nature of the science base: "Administrative relocation will not, however, improve the knowledge base, and, because risk assessment is only one element in the formulation of regulatory actions, even considerable improvements in risk assessment cannot be expected to eliminate controversy over these actions."[7] Following an analysis of the four federal agencies primarily responsible for regulating environmental risk—the Environmental Protection Agency, the Occupational Safety and Health Administration, the Food and Drug Administration, and the Consumer Product Safety Commission—the report recommended no sweeping administrative changes. However, recommendations were made for the development of uniform guidelines for use in the risk assessment process and for the establishment of a risk assessment methods board to assess the evolving scientific basis for risk assessment and to oversee the government's use of and research in the field of risk assessment.

The sources of scientific expertise

When expert scientific information is solicited, how can there be confidence that the evidence presented is valid? Should expert advice come from within the government or should it be drawn from the science community at large? The issue of scientific peer

7. NRC, *Risk Assessment*, p. 6.

review elicited a lively discussion at the workshop. The manner of choosing experts to provide advice to the government is of special concern in view of recent allegations that experts may have been selected for political and ideological reasons. In some agencies, scientific consultants serve on an appointment basis tied to changes in administrations, so that with a new administration, one set of consultants replaces another. A mechanism is needed to uncouple the selection of science experts from the political process. One suggestion was that a panel of experts, each serving fixed but staggered terms, might be instituted in place of the current practice. This would provide continuity of scientific and experiential expertise and minimize the likelihood of ideologues.

A companion issue is where the scientific data on which regulations are based should be generated. In May 1983 the public was scandalized by reports that a private testing laboratory, whose services were widely used by the chemical industry, had falsified much of its data. The implication was that numerous chemicals are regulated on the basis of invalid data, and the question of how to regulate chemicals took on a new urgency. Suggestions discussed included establishing an industry-sponsored safety testing institute, requiring more in-house testing by industry, and expanding the testing performed within government laboratories.

Any viable solution must separate testing responsibility from regulating responsibility and must minimize conflict-of-interest situations. Separation is especially important when the extreme fear is that toxic substances will cause cancer. There are two parts to toxicity testing: quantitative measurement of a chemical in biological or environmental samples and measurement of a chemical's biological effects at different concentrations. It is imperative that the quality of these measurements be assured by a government institution whose reputation inspires confidence. One government agency that provides state-of-the-art, independent measurement and standardization functions is the National Bureau of Standards (NBS).

The NBS develops reference standards and testing procedures and then provides measurement services. It abstains from interpreting the policy implications of its measurements. Although the government underwrites the development costs of tests and standards, users—government agencies and the private sector—pay for measurements on a fee-for-service basis. The NBS has fostered a mutually beneficial and productive interaction between government and industry. The NBS model should be considered in solving the problem of how government can assure competent testing and regulation of chemicals.

Another challenge is how best to foster scientific literacy in the general public. Public understanding of and confidence in environmental regulation requires some familiarity with the scientific issues involved. With increasing deregulation the consumer bears the burden of choice about whether or not to be exposed to the potential hazards of certain over-the-counter drugs or products like cigarettes and diet soft drinks that carry safety warnings. Scientific literacy is essential if the citizen is to choose wisely. Efforts to upgrade science education may encourage the development of such literacy.

The conceptual framework for risk assessment

Several of the addresses assembled reflect the workshop's struggle to formulate a framework for risk assessment. Such a conceptual framework can be discussed from many perspectives, most notably from a legislative, executive, or industrial point of view.

Dr. Thomas Moss, former staff director of the House Subcommittee on Science, Research, and Technology and now director of research administration and adjunct professor of physics at Carnegie-Mellon University, addressed the current legislative use of risk assessment in drafting regulatory legislation. He noted that there are three categories of regulatory statutes: one assessing risk only, the second considering technological feasibility, and the third seeking a balance between risks and benefits. Moss detected a trend in legislation toward balancing risks and costs, a trend that emphasizes the need to understand how best to use risk assessment. Taking as examples the Love Canal, Times Beach, and Canadian-U.S. acid rain controversies, he analyzed the positive and negative uses of scientific information in decisionmaking and pointed out what may be the hardest problem: the abuse of quantitative arguments in an adversarial climate.

A different perspective, that of a regulatory arm of the executive branch of government, was provided by Dr. J. Richard Crout, former director of the Bureau of Drugs at the FDA and now associate director for medical applications of research at the National Institutes of Health. By comparing and contrasting how benefit-risk analyses are employed for foods and drugs, he draws two different roles for the government in environmental regulation. In one—food regulation, for example, where the consumer has little choice in his exposure—the government's role is to set limits of safety. In the other—say, drugs, where the consumer has some choice in risk exposure—the aim of government policy should be to identify and publicize risk and to provide recommendations of restricted use.

He identified three areas where scientific information might improve regulatory policy: research to prevent unanticipated accidents, studies on individual susceptibility, and better development of the theory and concept of benefit-risk as exemplified by Lester Lave's recent work.[8]

Not all monitoring of environmental risk can or should be done only in response to government regulation. Speaking from an industrial perspective, Monte Throdahl, senior vice president for the Monsanto Company, indicated that industry should do more "self-regulation," especially for those chemicals that fall into the risk category in which the consumer cannot control his exposure. This idea represents a consensus of regulator and regulated.

Another consensus shared by the industrial and regulatory communities is that the Love Canal episode was an example of a "failure to properly apply science." This consensus, however, led to an issue that divided the workshop participants. Government representatives, whether from the Congress or the executive branch, favored linkage of the regulatory process and scientific assessment. This is also the position of the recent NRC report. In contrast, industry favored the establishment of a national science panel and a disjuncture of scientific judgment and regulatory formulation.

Detailed case studies of regulatory activity served to focus discussion on the options open to improve environmental regulation. The status of the Clean Air Act was assessed by Dr. Gilbert Omenn, dean of the School of Public Health at the University of Washington in Seattle. Dr. Omenn was discouraged because he saw no movement toward consensus or compromise to provide clean air standards or regulatory reform for hazardous air pollutants. Dr. Morton Corn, a former assistant secretary of labor for occupational health and safety, a consultant to many regulatory agencies, and currently a professor in and director of the division of environmental health engineering at Johns Hopkins University, assessed the regulatory climate for toxic waste and other toxic substances.

The current administration's effort to replace regulatory reform with weaker regulatory relief measures led to a shared concern by workshop participants that any slackening in the nation's efforts to protect the environment could lead to a future swing to over-regulation in subsequent administrations. Drastic shifts in policy incur significant costs, so continuity in policy is a sound aim.

8. Lester B. Lave, *Quantitative Risk Assessment in Regulation* (Brookings Institution, 1982).

Looking to the future

What are the areas in which new policies can achieve the common goal of sensitive and sensible environmental regulation? There was a consensus for improving scientific input into regulatory decisions and for improving the peer review system of advice to regulatory agencies. Increased participation by scientists in policy dialogues and a better communication of their work to the public were other agreed-on goals.

To achieve these goals requires more basic research both in biological science, to develop solid health-data baselines without which regulation is arbitrary, and in social science, to develop risk assessment as a discipline. There is also a need for scientific peer review of regulation as well as careful criticism of reports issued by research scientists.

Are new laws and institutions required to accomplish these goals, or do we need mainly to improve the enforcement and function of those that exist? Much debate ensued on this issue, but a majority favored enforcement of current statutes as the immediate priority.

The challenges articulated by the workshop participants—solicitation of expert opinion, use of risk-benefit analysis, improvement of the climate in which environmental regulations are established—are clear. The recommendations of the conference participants put forward in the addresses assembled here should provide an agenda from which more rational environmental policy can be formulated.

Differences in Assessing Risks for Food and Drugs

J. RICHARD CROUT

CHEMICAL RISKS fall into two categories that require different scientific and policy approaches. The first category consists of those situations in which an undesired (from the user's point of view), potentially hazardous compound is present in an essential substance; examples include food additives, air pollutants, and water contaminants. The individual has no choice about whether or not to take in the offending substance.

Our societal approach to risk management for hazards in essential substances is to limit exposure to a level deemed safe (a word I shall return to later) for everyone. Scientific efforts are directed toward identifying risks associated with chronic low-level exposure and toward estimating the probable degree of exposure of individuals. Policy emphasis is on public decision-making by Congress and the regulatory agencies, as these bodies decide, on behalf of the population at large, what individuals should be allowed to take in. Any benefit-risk formulation is complex and properly relates to society as a whole because those who benefit from the substance are sometimes different from those who take the risk. Furthermore, economic benefits must be balanced against health risks, an ever contentious policy dilemma.

The second category of chemical risk involves situations in which the risk is accepted as a consequence of the use of a product. The primary chemical example is drugs, although the risk associated with automobiles and many other consumer products is analogous. The elements of consumer choice and voluntary risk acceptance are fundamental to societal use of these sometimes high-risk products. Our risk-management strategy in this circumstance is to identify and quantify the risks as much as possible by providing information to the user through labeling or, in some cases, by restricting use (for example, prescription drugs). Scientific emphasis is placed on the accurate identification and quantification of hazards under the conditions of use. Policy focuses not only on public institutions but also on product labeling, consumer and professional education, and hazard surveillance in

10

the marketplace. A benefit-risk formulation in this instance relates to the individual who is both the beneficiary and the person at risk.

Food safety risks

The general safety standard for any food in the Food, Drug, and Cosmetic Act is that it shall not contain "any poisonous or deleterious substance which may render it injurious to health."[1] This was intended to cover toxins, poisons, heavy metals, and the like, that might find their way into food through spoilage, contamination, or other forms of adulteration. For additives intentionally placed in food for flavoring, coloring, or preservative purposes, the law specifies that an application for an additive may be disapproved "if a fair evaluation of data before the Secretary . . . fails to establish that the proposed use of the food additive, under the conditions of use . . . will be safe."[2] The well-known Delaney clause specifies further that "no additive shall be deemed to be safe if it is found to induce cancer when ingested by man or animal." The law further states that in deciding whether a proposed use of a food additive is safe, the secretary must consider the volume of consumption of the additive, the cumulative effects of the additive in the overall diet, and the opinion of scientific experts. Other provisions permit the setting of tolerances for pesticide residues and other contaminants that are inevitable consequences of modern agricultural practices.

The flavor of this legislative language, and the history of the administration of the food laws, has had the practical result of establishing the concept that the word "safe" means absolute safety. Though potentially dangerous chemicals are permitted in the food supply, tolerance levels well below those judged to be hazardous are the rule. In policy debates over the food laws, some suggest that a concept of "societally acceptable risk" or "insignificant risk" should be substituted for the word "safe." Whether this would have any practical effect on the administration of the law is unclear.

Scientific studies intended to assess the risks posed by food additives and pesticides are oriented toward investigating toxicological mechanisms and metabolism and toward identifying safety thresholds. Scientists seek to determine the maximum dose of the substance that fails to produce observable toxicological effects in animals. Tolerance levels are then set by dividing this

1. 21 U.S.C. 342.
2. 21 U.S.C. 348.

exposure level by an arbitrary but empirically successful factor, such as 100. With the advent of modern biochemical toxicology and of comparative studies of the metabolism of foreign compounds in animals and man, increasing sophistication has been brought to the estimation of risk levels in humans. But the fundamental approach, like that used for environmental contaminants, is to identify an upper exposure level that is considered safe.

Drug safety risk

The situation with drugs is considerably different even though the statutory safety standards look remarkably similar. The drug law provides that an application for a new drug shall be disapproved if, among other things, the studies presented do not "show whether or not such drug is safe for use under the conditions prescribed, recommended, or suggested in the proposed labeling thereof,"[3] or "the results of such tests show that such drug is unsafe for use under such conditions or do not show that such drug is safe for use under such conditions."[4] This language has historically been interpreted as requiring decisionmaking on the basis of the benefit-risk principle. The word "safe" was not taken in isolation; instead, the phrase "safe for use under the conditions prescribed . . . in the proposed labeling" was taken in its entirety as the governing statement. Similarly, the benefit that is recognized is the use mentioned in the label. There has been some debate about changing the safety standard in the drug law. However, the discussion has centered largely on making the benefit-risk language more explicit, not on changing the basic interpretation of the safety standard.

Risk assessment studies for drugs are designed to identify the side effects and potential hazards that accompany use of a drug in the treatment of a particular disease or condition. Acute, subacute, and sometimes chronic testing of investigational drugs is done in animals before their clinical evaluation in humans. The main objectives of the animal studies are to define the toxicological properties of the drug, to guide clinical investigators in selecting the initial doses to be evaluated in humans, to aid the monitoring of toxicity, and to elucidate toxicological mechanisms.

As clinical experience with a new drug expands, the data collected in humans become, with two exceptions, the major knowledge base for risk assessment at the time of approval. The two exceptions are the animal studies done to assess carcinogenic

3. 21 U.S.C. 355.
4. Ibid.

and teratogenic risks, neither of which can be evaluated definitively in humans for technical and ethical reasons.

After a new drug has been approved and marketed, the exposure of patients to the drug typically expands by orders of magnitude over the number exposed during the investigational phase. Adverse reactions are now closely monitored to identify previously undetected problems. In time, epidemiological studies may become available on carcinogenic or teratogenic risks, information that for technical reasons is far more difficult, if not impossible, to obtain for food additives and environmental contaminants.

An important feature of the drug law is that it permits drugs that vary widely in their toxicity to be marketed. Some drugs used for the treatment of cancer, for example, are highly toxic to vital organs and may even be carcinogenic. But because of the seriousness of the disease and the lack of alternatives, such drugs may be approved on benefit-risk grounds. On the other hand, a similar degree of toxicity would not be permitted for tranquilizers, analgesics, or antihypertensive drugs, because much safer alternatives are available. All drugs nevertheless carry some degree of risk. As such, they are the only chemicals intentionally given to humans at doses that may carry risk of adverse side effects, injury, or death.

Science and public policy, health, and the environment

Among the many policy debates to which better scientific information would contribute effectively, I would emphasize three.

The first is the role of research in preventing unanticipated, dreaded accidents. Such episodes are typified by thalidomide, cyanide in Tylenol, dioxin in the soil, and the threatened meltdown at Three Mile Island. These accidents have an enormous effect on public attitudes and public policy, an effect sometimes disproportionate to their epidemiological significance. While we will never be able to foresee every problem of this type, we can improve our anticipatory capabilities in risk identification. Basic toxicological research on in-vitro and animal predictors of human toxicity, and improved epidemiological surveillance to identify chemical accidents as soon as possible, would help tremendously.

A second important area to be investigated is individual variation in susceptibility to specific chemical risks. An important principle of risk management is that people will accept responsibility for personal risk if given information and control over the decision. Health care will be increasingly influenced by this principle as medical decisionmaking moves from physician dominance to a more shared relationship with patients.

If people are to assume greater personal responsibility for

protecting themselves from environmental risks, they must have accurate information on their susceptibility to harm from environmental agents like cigarettes, chemicals in the work place, and particular foods and drugs. People show a wide variation in their metabolism rates for certain drugs. There is every reason to believe that the current explosion in genetic research will ultimately unravel why some people are more likely than others to get, say, cancer or emphysema in response to such noxious agents as cigarette smoke or sulfur dioxide. If each of us had a profile of his or her genetic susceptibilities and resistances, we could adopt individualized preventive strategies. Research studies that might foster this goal include:

—basic biomedical research on the genetic and environmental factors that account for individual sensitivity to drugs and foreign compounds;

—studies on the mechanism of individual variation in the metabolism of drugs and foreign compounds;

—pharmacokinetic and mechanism studies in humans of the interaction among foods, drugs, and foreign compounds;

—studies on the influence of disease states on individual sensitivity to foreign compounds; and

—basic and applied research on vaccines, drugs, and gene therapies that might fundamentally alter individual susceptibility to foreign compounds.

A third area for public policy research is the benefit-risk concept itself. The principle of balancing the desirable against the undesirable pervades every policy decision made in this area by government or individuals. Nevertheless, there has been relatively little research, either theoretical or applied, aimed at identifying how we use, or ought to use, the benefit-risk principle in decisionmaking. The relative contributions to decisions of scientific data and value judgments are not well quantified. The attitude of the public toward certain risks is not well documented, and the way these attitudes are formed is poorly understood. In the absence of dispassionate and meticulously collected research data, advocacy groups, the media, and the politically strong have a disproportionate influence on policy decisions.

Four areas that might benefit from social- and behavioral-sciences research are: improved modeling of the benefit-risk process; broad assessment of public attitudes toward risk taking in various circumstances; basic research on why people accept or reject particular risks; and evaluation of various risk assessment processes for potentially hazardous chemicals, food additives, and drugs.

I do not foresee that this research agenda will be accomplished quickly. However, over the next generation scientists will undoubtedly make substantial progress in offering to policymakers and individuals a far wider range of possibilities for risk management than we now possess. I suspect that for some this research agenda may be oriented too little toward risk identification and risk avoidance, our classical approach. I do not undervalue this important and essential strategy for risk management. But I do suggest that the future, properly orchestrated, could include a modestly improved capability for anticipating and preventing chemical disasters, a vastly improved understanding of individual variation in susceptibility to environmental risks, and a much improved understanding of the theory and practice of the benefit-risk process. Increasing opportunities will therefore be available for people to adopt personal preventive strategies to supplement our usual population-oriented public health approach. These may include such means to increase individual resistance as vaccines, drugs, or genetic therapies, as well as the well-established approach of risk avoidance. The availability of a diverse set of tools for risk management should be encouraged as we move toward an ever more complex world of foreign substances in our environment.

Risk Assessment
and the Legislative Process

THOMAS H. MOSS

THE KEY to retaining one's sanity while viewing how risk analysis is used in the legislative process is probably to adopt the idea that one is looking at a rich and healthy social experiment in action. From this viewpoint the inconsistencies, stops and starts, and variations in approach look like a Darwinian struggle for survival among competing ways of handling risk analysis. The greater the diversity, the more varied the results and the greater the informational value of the "grand experiment." Of course, if one is a legal purist or a scientist seeking truth and consistency, things may look quite bleak and frustrating. Risk analysis is obviously a kind of social "experiential learning," and everyone must draw his conclusions about the experience from his own personal viewpoint.

I would like to examine the diversity and implications of various legislative risk assessment approaches. A central point is to recognize that, for better or for worse, risk assessment is now a powerful part of the legislative and political process: however imperfect things may be, it is not possible to turn back the political clock and to wait until scientific and institutional mechanisms are in better shape. Our task is to make the best of what we have while seeking incremental improvements. In that task we may learn by reviewing the case histories of recent years.

In the 1960s and 1970s public concern rose over such health and environmental threats as toxic chemicals, depletion of the ozone layer, nuclear accidents, and waste disposal. Indeed, the Delaney clause, added in 1958 to the Food, Drug, and Cosmetic Act, set the stage for many regulatory battles in the ensuing two decades. The Delaney clause was the prototype of one of three distinct categories of risk-oriented regulatory legislation. The three categories are risk only, technological feasibility, and balanced cost versus risk.

Some legislation, like the Delaney clause, involves risk-only criteria. Specified risks trigger action automatically, regardless of costs or benefits. Under such legislation the regulatory agency is given almost no latitude for judgment in its actions once any level of risk is detected.

Other statutes contain provisions involving the concept of technological feasibility. In section 111 of the Clean Air Act of 1977, for example, the mandate is for pollutant emission reductions "achievable through application of the best technological system of continuous emission reduction."

Finally, more recent regulatory laws allow a balancing of costs versus risks and benefits. The Toxic Substances Control Act is one example. In section 5(c) the act requires that, before promulgating any rule about a chemical substance or mixture subject to review by the Environmental Protection Agency, the administrator must consider not only the effects of the substance or mixture on human health and the environment but also "the benefits of such substance or mixture to various uses and the availability of substitutes for such uses, and the reasonably ascertainable economic consequences of the rule."

Of the thirty-four pieces of major regulatory legislation currently in force, seven are based on risk-only criteria, two on the best-available-technology approach, and twenty-five on some notion of balancing risks and costs. Thus although the absolute criterion of the Delaney clause has received much attention, the balancing approach is the most common mechanism in regulatory law.

There was a clear and distinct change in attitude in favor of balancing approaches in the 1970s. This is most vividly seen in the contrast between the Clean Air Act of 1970 and the amendments of 1977. In committee reports and court decisions based on the 1970 act, public health was explicitly viewed as an absolute. However, during the action on the 1977 amendments, the legislation was embellished with dozens of requirements aimed at balancing health protection goals against costs, adverse economic consequences, and technical difficulties. This changing attitude and the predominance of statutes with the balancing approach show that risk analysis is a reality of the legislative process, a reality that must be faced by both the scientific and political communities.

I have three general observations on the current use of risk analysis in the political arena.

First, it is foolish not to use the best quantitative risk assessments available in forming public policy on health, the environment, and safety protection. However, risk assessment is no substitute for experienced, well-balanced judgment involving many complex factors outside the realm of risk quantification. If risk assessment is used as a crutch to avoid facing the need for judgment on complex nonquantitative issues, chaos and confusion are likely to result.

Second, though the scientific community has welcomed the use of risk assessment as a victory for the quantitative approach to issues, its use represents an enormous challenge to the resources and organizational ability of that community. It is not clear whether scientists will or should rise to the challenge.

Third, the credibility of risk assessment in decisionmaking has been a victim of the adversarial climate created by the protagonists in public health and environmental debates. To a large extent regulated industries, advocacy groups, and scientists themselves have chosen and created that climate. It is now coming back to haunt them and society as a whole.

I believe what is needed is a commitment to absolute honesty and a respect for the ability of the public and the political community to integrate facts and judgments into an overall understanding of policy needs.

Before expanding on these observations, I want to note that the House Subcommittee on Science, Research, and Technology has tried to promote the idea of risk assessment as an important, developing technology for the decisionmaking process. To make this point the committee has held hearings and seminars, often in collaboration with scientific groups. In its last session, Congress had before it a piece of legislation called the Risk Analysis Research and Demonstration Act, which was originally introduced by Congressman Don Ritter of Pennsylvania. This legislation was not directly involved in the various regulatory debates then raging; it sought instead to introduce a sense of quality control and to promote systematic improvements in risk assessment applications. The bill was passed last year by the House, but narrowly missed enactment in the last days of the session. It is likely to be reintroduced this year with considerable momentum already behind it.

A few case histories illustrate the three observations I made above. The first concerned the difficulty of blending commonsense judgment and quantitative scientific factors in decisionmaking. One of the most vivid examples was the controversy surrounding the decision to evacuate the residents of Love Canal, New York, as opposed to the more recent EPA buy-out offer to the residents of dioxin-contaminated Times Beach, Missouri. Neither of these actions was the result of legislative decisions, but both were colored by political forces operating informally in the legislative process.

The Love Canal incident was, I believe, a real setback to the use of risk assessment in public policy. It was also a setback to public respect for the government's ability to protect public health and safety. I do not fault the final decision to evacuate the residents. That was a perfectly defensible, conservative move to protect public health, and it was well within the tradition of decisions made by public health officers faced with threats of unknown dimensions. What was tragic was the ill-fated attempt to link the decision to a fragmentary and poorly controlled chromosome-breakage analysis. The direct association, at a press conference, of the chromosome-breakage evidence with the decision to evacuate compromised the integrity of scientific risk approaches to the issue. It also made a mockery of the integrity of the EPA decisionmaking process. The chromosome-breakage results were not sufficiently detailed, comprehensive, or controlled; the scientific evidence was not complete enough to justify the decision.

What could have justified the EPA action was the acknowledgement that there was a risk of frankly unknown and unknowable (on a short time scale) magnitude. The reliance on fragmentary, pseudoscientific evidence confused what otherwise might have been a widely respected decision. The incident reflects the unfortunate tendency to use science to avoid traditional obligations for sound public policy judgments.

In contrast to Love Canal, the recent decision on Times Beach seemed to reflect a lesson learned. While there may have been excessive delay, we were not deceived into thinking that we could wait for complete dose-response knowledge or for positive indications of adverse health effects before acting. The EPA recognized that risk analysis could not dictate the course in the Times Beach case, and it acted on common sense. The question is not one of ignoring or undervaluing facts and scientific evidence, but of simply recognizing the limitations of risk assessment and the need for action.

The fluorocarbon-ozone controversy was one that I think reflects a positive interaction of scientific notions of risk with nonscientific public policy judgments. In the 1977 amendments to the Clean Air Act, Congress resisted the temptation to simply ban or limit the use of fluorocarbons despite a good deal of sensationalist clamor. But it likewise resisted industry attempts to ridicule and bury the emerging evidence. Congress wisely chose to rely on a timed evaluation of the emerging data by the National Academy of Sciences. The study was not mandated as a temporizing device, and it explicitly required a public decision by the EPA administrator at the end of a specified time. What I respect in this approach is the explicit recognition that the evidence really needed to be considered and integrated once more before action was taken. However, once the study was over, there was a commitment to action on a best-judgment basis, regardless of the inevitable incompleteness of the data.

In many ways the congressional override of the saccharin ban falls into a class similar to the fluorocarbon-ozone case, with the regulatory decision going the opposite way. Congress looked hard at the scientific evidence linking saccharin with bladder cancer. Although it was not prepared to generally overrule the basically conservative thrust of the Delaney clause, in this specific case it judged that important nonscientific factors made the saccharin risk acceptable and the ban inadvisable.

My second observation concerns the burden facing the scientific community in meeting demands for implementing risk assessment in the legislative process. The important discovery of biological methylation as an unexpected transport mechanism for environmental mercury is one small example of the thousands of complex mechanisms of health and environmental stress that must be understood in order to fulfill the optimistic hopes for risk assessment. Understanding the potential ecological impact of carbon dioxide is a large-scale example of the same burden. Integrating vast amounts of diverse technical data into a credible statement that can be used to judge the need for changes in our energy and agricultural strategies presents a historic challenge to the scientific community. Scientists may find the demands for detailed data and repeated verification oppressive. Skills in organization, data management, and technique standardization may become more highly sought than the traditionally valued virtues relating to individual achievement and scientific anarchy.

Another challenge for the scientific community is to actively promote public understanding of the many factors involved in risk assessment. Scientists involved in recombinant DNA research have shown, perhaps, the most sensitivity toward this need in having developed voluntary guidelines and having promoted public participation in local university committees and innovative institutions like the Cambridge Citizens Council. Declining scientific literacy among the general public foretells even greater abuse of both judgment and science in reaching policy decisions. Such a decline could be fatal to both the policy process and the

scientific community itself, and scientists must not wait for someone else to take steps to reverse the trend.

My third observation concerns the adversarial climate in which risk assessment often takes place. On many key issues, there has been a pattern of participants balancing precariously between a problem-solving approach and one characterized by selective treatment of the facts, exaggerated claims, and ridicule—rather than honest consideration—of opponents' views. Controversies over the ozone, lead, nitrites, tobacco, meat and cholesterol, acid rain, and many other issues have shown this delicate balance.

Unfortunately, individuals and groups are often motivated to choose the adversarial approach in the belief that this is the only way to win in public policy forums. Too frequently this is true in the short term. However, continuing to pander to the worst aspects of public policy is to do long-range damage to the credibility of science in public policy formation. Such actions feed on the gaps in public scientific literacy and sow the seeds for further disenchantment with and alienation from scientific reasoning.

The controversy over whether to include acid rain issues in the attempted 1981–82 rewrite of the Clean Air Act was one of the most horrifying examples of how a problem-solving policy approach can degenerate into an adversarial process. By 1980 it was clear that increasingly acidic rain was becoming a real problem in the Northeast United States and Eastern Canada. It was also clear that the origin of the phenomenon was complex and that the optimal control strategy was uncertain. Had industry and environmental groups been willing to accept these premises, I believe an intelligent control strategy could have been developed in a reasonably short period of time. However, after flirting with the idea of a reasoned problem-solving approach, the opposing groups decided to go for the political jugular, choosing a win-lose strategy instead of a win-win accommodation.

The coal and utility industries published reams of glossy material ridiculing available scientific findings, the smug assumption being that uncertainty and incompleteness in the data meant that acid rain concerns should simply be forgotten for another several years. The simple notion of building timed decision points into scientific programs was fought as premature and "unwarranted by the facts." On the other hand, many environmental groups decided that acid rain should be used as a political club in the overall debate on amendments to the Clean Air Act. The demand for immediate action on acid rain control became a powerful rallying point, and it was pressed with an urgency that belied the uncertainty of acid rain's determinants and the inertia of the atmospheric and terrestrial-energy ecosystems.

Both sides chose short-range political goals at the risk of their own long-range integrity and, in my opinion, self-interest. The pressure for control strategies for acid rain is inexorable. Industry, in taking a "Let's ridicule the evidence" stance, instead of a "Let's work together and get to the root of the problem" approach, put itself in a position in which it would have little credibility or influence in determining an eventual well-reasoned solution. Similarly, in seeking to sensationalize the issue for maximum immediate regulatory effect, the environmental side set the stage for a backlash of public skepticism if the urgently demanded control strategies later turned out to be costly investments missing the true needs. The tragic "tall stack" solution to controlling local sulfur deposition was just such a skepticism-building and costly misguided investment.

There are many other examples of the pervasiveness and danger of adversary science. An informal estimates paper on cancer incidence from the Department of Health, Education, and Welfare became the source of articles talking of a cancer epidemic caused by industrial pollutants or chemical food additives. These spawned a series of retaliatory pamphlets by industry ridiculing some of the HEW projections and going on to gloss over some very real hazards in the work place. The current debate over the significance of genotoxic versus epigenetic causes of cancer is reminiscent of similar debates over the toxicity of ionizing radiation, in which different risk standards were considered for different forms of radiation. In both cases some on the opposing scientific sides leapt prematurely and seized upon new data as an excuse to move away from established conservative public health standards. The net effect in both cases was to erode public confidence in the authority of scientific findings and to create an image that public health standards depend on attention to daily developments in the nation's laboratories. A less adversarial and more tempered use of new data and ideas could have promoted a picture of scientific authority as something that continually changes, adjusts to new findings, and allows for a free and open discussion of the possible need to change conventional wisdom, all the while recognizing that established health standards must have a built-in conservatism that transcends short-term scientific debates.

The counterproductivity of the adversarial route is perhaps most clearly shown by the Reagan administration's loss of credibility in environmental and health-protection policy. The 1980 election provided a public mandate and a golden opportunity to rationalize the setting of health and environmental standards in this country. Some regulatory approaches clearly had proved to be much less effective than others in providing health and environmental protection, and new scientific data had altered the assumptions underlying others. A quiet and scientifically solid approach to seeking appropriate revisions in regulatory law and policy could have gathered broad support and brought both political and technical-economic rewards. However, by allowing its approaches to regulatory reform to be encumbered by strong ideological and adversarial extremes, the administration tragically disenfranchised itself as a credible partner in true problem-solving approaches. In fact it has probably set the stage for another backlash of excessive zeal in environmental regulation, with the public assuming that weakened agencies such as the EPA can no longer be trusted or relied on to protect public concerns.

It is perhaps strange to leave the citadel of cynicism that is Washington and Congress with some of the attitudes I have spoken of. But moral or philosophical judgments aside, I believe that trust, directness, candor, and acknowledgement of limitations are the most *utilitarian* of virtues in the arena of risk assessment, as they are in many other areas. The effectiveness of many of the most respected and influential individuals and groups I knew while in Congress was more dependent on consistent credibility and a willingness to seek win-win problem-solving approaches than on clever and seemingly effective debating tricks. There will always be tempting and seemingly politically astute advice on shading or selectively presenting the facts or exaggerating their significance. A political victory may seem to be at hand if a few people can be persuaded by one's overstepping the line where science stops and other kinds of judgment begin. But my experience tells me that when scientists or politicians fall prey to this temptation in the area of risk assessment, they destroy not only themselves as players in the political process but also the truly useful tool of risk assessment.

In many ways the individual controversies over risk assessment and public policy are minidramas in the overall evolution of our attitudes toward risk. Many of us have played in these dramas and will need to choose future roles as problem solvers, adversaries, mediators, ridiculers, and so on. The interests of science, the public, regulated groups, and public policy activists will be severely damaged if we do not escape the adversarial roles in our respective dramas.

Science and Environmental Risk: Policy Issues

DENIS PRAGER

MY COMMENTS on the role of science in determining and regulating environmental risk fall into two main categories: substantive issues and process issues. Under the substantive issues category, four important themes have been touched on during this workshop: the future of risk analysis, the future of risk-benefit analysis, the question of who decides what constitutes acceptable risk, and the question of the separation of science and decisionmaking.

Risk analysis and risk-benefit analysis

Risk analysis, or risk characterization, is usually viewed as the final step in the scientific phase of the regulatory process. By that point scientists have, to the degree permitted by available data, characterized a risk and then stepped aside and said, "This is what we know about this situation; now it is up to you politicians or decisionmakers to make the regulatory decisions."

It seems clear that risk assessment will be an increasingly valuable tool. Although it is not now highly developed, and many of us have concerns about the way it is sometimes used and often viewed as a panacea, there is an increasing demand for scientists to characterize risks better and to describe them in quantitative terms on which people can depend. One problem I see is that people are already tending to depend on risk assessment more than they should. Many on Capitol Hill see risk assessment as a panacea. This concerns me because it masks the pervasive inadequacy of data and the many judgment calls involved in regulatory science. In most cases the scientific data base for a potential risk is poor, and scientists are forced to make many judgment calls along the way. Often nonscientists view science as judgment free, absolutely quantitative, and objective. Calls for science panels and science courts often imply that simply getting a group of eminent scientists around a table ensures clear, distinct decisions about the health risks of particular hazards. Many of us realize that this is simply not the case; in this arena yes-or-no, black-and-white decisions seldom exist.

Once scientists have presented their assessment of the nature

24

of a particular risk, the responsible regulator must (if permitted by law) make a regulatory decision based on a balance between the risks and benefits of various alternatives. It seems clear from such visible cases as benzene and cotton dust that we are moving toward greater rather than lesser reliance on the use of risk-benefit analysis in deciding important regulatory issues. Most of us seem to view risk-benefit analysis as controversial and contentious. Yet in the area of drugs, as Richard Crout explained, risk-benefit analysis always has been inherent in the process of approving and using drugs. Where the benefit of a chemical product—a drug—is improved health, we seem willing to accept considerable risk. This is an important area of regulation where risks and benefits have been balanced all along.

But how will society identify the benefits of other consumer products like agricultural chemicals, steel, autos, petrochemicals, and energy? What are the benefits in terms of jobs, exports, tax revenues, and quality of life against which we can compare risks? This is in large measure what we are trying to get at when we talk about the risks of occupational and environmental exposures and the need to know the benefits against which to judge them. As Lester Lave has suggested, we may be better off talking about risk-risk analysis than risk-benefit analysis.

Who decides what constitutes acceptable risk?

Unfortunately the issue is much different when the benefit of balancing a risk is not improved health, and we are forced to ask the question, "In the many complex risk-benefit dilemmas we face, who will decide for the public what constitutes acceptable risk?" It has been suggested that the public should have the opportunity to express its viewpoint about risks and benefits. But if we are going to ask our citizens to make such decisions, they will have to be much more sophisticated than they are now. Further, we as scientists and public policy figures will have to go to greater lengths to educate the public about risks and about the way in which risks can be compared. That is the basic intent of the legislation that Congressman Don Ritter has been promoting for the last four years. His proposed legislation attempts to get the federal government to do a better job of providing the public with information about the way in which one risk compares with another. That is not what the bill says directly, but that is what Mr. Ritter intends. He says that people ought to be able to make benefit-risk decisions themselves and that perhaps the main function of the government is to provide them with the information they need to do so.

The whole question of voluntary versus involuntary risks has been raised in this workshop again and again. To me this issue defines the paradoxical nature of our approach to controlling risks to public health. We concentrate vigorously on involuntary risks—those related to occupational and environmental pollutants, primarily chemicals. Yet at the regulatory level, we pay much less attention to those risk factors that we can control ourselves—smoking, drinking, and driving, for example—since they are related to life-style choices. We defer to "freedom of choice" and "freedom of expression," but the fact is that if we made more sensible decisions about cigarettes, alcohol, speed limits, the use of seat belts, and the like, the effect on public health would be so tremendous as to make seem insignificant the effect of many of the regulatory decisions over which we struggle so hard.

Separating science from decisionmaking

The last substantive issue is the question of separating science from decisionmaking. I am not exactly sure how much of an issue this really is. The real question is not whether we separate science from decisionmaking but how we do so. Everybody wants to see at least some separation. We want to see scientists do the best possible job of bringing the information together so that policymakers can make use of it; we want to see the actual decisions made by politicians who are put into their jobs to reflect the political will of the people.

Perhaps the best approach to separating science from decisionmaking is to improve the science. One reason there isn't more of a separation is that in many cases the data base is simply not credible. Strengthening the quality of the science to the point that risk characterizations are reliable and credible will increase the degree to which decisionmakers are willing to accept those characterizations as the principal basis for regulatory decisions.

Process issues

My comments on the second category—process issues—reflect my experience in the Office of Science and Technology Policy over the past five years. I believe strongly that the Reagan administration came in with a mandate to do something long-term, permanent, and sensible about rationalizing the regulatory process, and I am one of many in the administration who feel uneasy about our failure to take advantage of that mandate. I lay the blame primarily on the executive office rather than on the agencies. We have failed to establish the framework and provide the leadership necessary to develop and implement a strategy for bringing about real change in the process whereby needed regulations are formulated and promulgated. What would I do to bring about such change? I would address three areas: testing, research, and decisionmaking.

First, I would remove the federal government from the business of testing chemicals. We now spend hundreds of millions of taxpayer dollars testing compounds because we don't trust the private sector to do the testing itself. We can and must develop mechanisms, such as those used in the area of drugs, that assure public confidence in private-sector testing of chemicals.

Second, I would reorganize the way in which regulatory research is done in the federal government. In my scheme regulatory agencies would not have major research capabilities themselves but would depend on a central research capability for long-term, basic regulatory science. I would allow each regulatory agency a relatively limited budget for technical assistance. That money would be spent primarily for providing technical assistance (monitoring, measurement, analysis, and quality control) to the regulatory side of the agency so that it could do its job better.

I would establish an office of regulatory science to direct and coordinate research common to the needs of all regulatory agencies. The office of regulatory research would be responsible for intramural or extramural long-term research done through the National Institutes of Health (NIH). The office would be placed either in the Department of Health and Human Services under the assistant secretary for health, or in the Executive Office of the President under the science adviser. The office of regulatory research would sponsor and stimulate appropriate research at NIH, conduct basic regulatory science through the National Center for Toxicological Research, and provide test development and validation through the National Toxicology Program.

I would also move as quickly as possible to change completely the way in which we approach regulatory decisionmaking. The current process is basically adversarial. We know in advance that almost every significant issue will end up in the courts, and so we start with the most extreme positions. I would move toward a consensus position as early as possible in the regulatory process, that is, as soon as a problem is identified. Three or four years ago we identified formaldehyde as a potential problem. At that point we should have established a process involving the federal government, state governments, interest groups, labor, and industry to develop a consensus on the risk to human health of exposure to formaldehyde. That would have brought together all interested parties as early in the process as possible to develop the knowledge on which to base regulatory decisions. I think we are ready for this now. People are weary of the adversarial process. The Reagan administration has tried to tilt the regulatory apparatus toward less burdensome regulation. If in the 1984 election a Democratic administration were to come in, there would be a backlash so severe that the situation might completely reverse. Unless we move toward a consensus process, we will play political handball forever with little benefit to the environment or to public health.

Regulating Toxic Substances: An Update

MORTON CORN

THE TERM "toxic waste disposal" implies more than the getting rid of hazardous chemical wastes through such means as high-temperature incineration, ground burial or encapsulation, or ocean incineration dumping. Toxic waste disposal suggests all the pathways by which a highly industrial or postindustrial society rids itself of potentially hazardous chemical compounds it cannot use or use economically. Thus disposal to air and water, as well as disposal of hazardous wastes after processing, is toxic waste disposal.

We have attempted to control chemicals in the United States through various federal regulatory statutes. Between 1965 and 1979 fifteen regulatory laws were passed by Congress (as opposed to only two between 1938 and 1965). All these laws were vigorously enforced during the period 1976–80. Indeed, what many considered overzealous enforcement created the issue of regulatory reform, one of the main concerns of the Reagan administration. The volume and detail of regulations promulgated by agencies charged with enforcing these laws led the private sector to demand less regulation. Since its inception the Reagan administration has been engaged in regulatory reform, or regulatory relief, depending on one's vantage point.

Superfund

Beleaguered EPA administrator Anne McGill Burford and Superfund administrator Rita M. Lavelle were among the first to go after allegations of misconduct in Superfund enforcement. It was charged that many sweetheart deals were made with the private sector and that favoritism was rampant, issues that I cannot address here because there has been only limited release of information relevant to Superfund activity.

We do know that $220 million of Superfund money was spent on five abandoned dump sites, and that approximately $150 million was recovered from the firms involved. We also know that with allocations-per-site estimated on the basis of expenditures to date, only 170 of the estimated 14,000 waste sites that are

29

candidates for cleanup will be financed through the Superfund. At this point there is approximately $53.6 million of unaccounted-for Superfund money. After months of delay, the EPA announced on February 22, 1983, that it would spend approximately $40 million of Superfund money to "buy back" dioxin-contaminated homes and land from residents of Times Beach, Missouri. Agency observers viewed this as a face-saving and diversionary decision made at the height of congressional investigation of Superfund activity, an action hastily and reluctantly taken. It is noteworthy that not one dollar of Superfund money has been allocated to investigations of the possible adverse health effects of waste sites.

At this point, at least three congressional committees are examining how Superfund sites were selected and how expenditures for cleanup were made. I fear that the coming months will reveal in excruciating detail the glacial progress of Superfund implementation. Though we may hope that all allegations of irregularities are untrue, that wish borders on starry-eyed optimism at this point. A major political scandal appears to be in progress and, almost needless to say, the effect on morale at the EPA has been devastating.

The Toxic Substance Control Act

The EPA's rather lax enforcement of environmental statutes can be more easily documented than the Superfund story, where records are being withheld or allegedly have been destroyed. Witness what has happened in the past two years as regards the Toxic Substance Control Act (TSCA). The act was designed to control hazardous chemicals entering commerce and to deal with existing chemicals with hazardous properties. There are record-keeping, reporting, and testing requirements under the act.

Under section 5E, the premanufacture regulatory notification clause of the act, only one chemical—a benzidine dye imported from Japan—has been acted upon. The agency is pursuing only one action—seeking approximately $1 million in fines from five companies. In contrast, there were eight premanufacture actions during the time between the passage of the act in 1977 and July 1979. Thus, as judged by actions on new chemicals, there has been only one-eighth the regulatory activity under section 5E during the Reagan administration as there was in the last years of the Carter presidency. Approximately 1,000 5E applications arrive at the EPA every year. If the EPA does not act upon these applications within ninety days, the manufacturer can proceed with production. A positive agency response is required to prevent production. Thus one way to achieve "regulatory reform" without changing the law is to reduce agency staff, thereby making it more difficult to react within the ninety-day response period. In February 1983 the TSCA support staff numbered approximately 360; in 1980 there were more than 500 TSCA staff members.

A proposed significant new-use rule was ready at the time the Reagan administration took office; it was withdrawn. Two new ones were proposed in February 1983.

Under section 4 of the act, there was a court-imposed schedule to an interagency testing agreement. Of those points that the EPA has responded to, it has concluded that most do not require testing; the few remaining ones industry has agreed to independently test.

Section 6 of the act regulates existing chemicals. The EPA has finalized the proposal for the identification and notification of asbestos. These requirements are strictly in relation to asbestos in schools. The Department of Education has issued regulations governing asbestos in school systems; EPA provides technical assistance. Other than for asbestos, there has been no new regulation of any existing chemical under section 6 during the Reagan administration.

Under section 8 of the act (recordkeeping and reporting), only two actions have been taken. During the Carter administration there was a proposal for gathering information applicable to approximately 2,300 chemicals. The chemicals chosen included some in line for regulation by the Interagency Testing Committee and others for which "substantial risk notifications" would have been required.

A recordkeeping proposal by the Carter administration has not been approved. Neither have proposals for testing or regulation of ethylene dichloride.

Finally, as staff members of the Toxic Substances Office have left the agency, their places have been taken by senior people displaced from the Pesticides Office by program cuts there. This further slows down efforts to implement the law because technically knowledgeable, young and enthusiastic personnel have been replaced by older senior personnel unfamiliar with the TSCA.

Outside the EPA

A similar picture, though different in details, emerges for the Occupational Safety and Health Administration (OSHA), which is charged with protecting the health and well-being of workers. The situation at the Consumer Products Safety Commission is no better. It is clear that the Reagan administration has attempted to curtail the issuance and enforcement of all but minor health, safety, and environmental regulations. Not one new health standard has emerged from OSHA during the past two years; staff is committed to rewriting those already promulgated. We are experiencing a hiatus in environmental regulation in the United States. The administration is committed to transferring environmental responsibilities to the states; unfortunately, there are proposed funding reductions to states of 25 percent for pollution control programs. Proposed budget cuts in federal water, air, and drinking-water programs range from 10 to 55 percent. In addition, there have been efforts to place cost-benefit requirements on regulations scheduled to take effect. The cost-benefit balance can provide a rationale for further inaction.

It is only to be expected that an executive branch appointee, generally in disagreement with the mission of an agency, will fail to implement the law in an appropriate manner and according to a reasonable timetable. Regulatory reform is not necessarily regulatory relief, and it is certainly not regulatory curtailment. I suspect the current subterfuges for undermining environmental statutes will eventually be exposed. Those of us professionally committed to environmental management will be left with a mammoth rebuilding effort.

This appraisal has not been optimistic, but that was not my intent. I am portraying the situation as it exists and expressing my concerns.

New Scientific Issues

ROBERT J. MOOLENAAR

IN PREPARING for this symposium, I checked my usual sources of information to identify new scientific issues. Going through recent issues of various American Chemical Society journals, I found lots of reports concerning new science discoveries, but not one new science policy issue. In contrast, in reading the *New York Times* and the *Washington Post,* I found science policy issues on almost every page, but with them was very little scientific detail. My intent here is to draw together the issues and the science that underlies them, to address the question of whether our government is capable of dealing with both in a manner that fulfills its role as the servant of the people. When Solomon observed that "there is nothing new under the sun" (Ecclesiastes 1:9), he may have been suffering from the "we've tried that" syndrome of old age, although his focus was on the world's mysteries rather than man's discovery process. But we actually generate little that is really new, though we continually gain insight into how the world is constructed and functions.

Years later Cicero presented another perspective when he noted, "Nothing quite new is perfect." It often takes a long time for theories and postulates to become thoroughly understood and to gain the status of scientific law. And later Niccolò Machiavelli observed in *The Prince,* "There is nothing more difficult to take in hand, more perilous to conduct, or more uncertain in its success, than to take the lead in the introduction of a new order of things." Clearly, the effects of man's social innovations were appreciated even in Machiavelli's day. The law of inertia, discovered by Newton for the physical world, seems to have been discovered by Machiavelli with respect to man's mind.

In recent years a more positive attitude has developed concerning new concepts and ideas. We live now in a world of instant happenings, ranging from the development of and solution to complex problems as conveyed in half-hour TV programs to viewing firsthand in our own living rooms man's exploration of the moon. Such acceptance of new developments is particularly true in the technical-industrial world, where new ideas are commonly—and rapidly—developed into usable technology.

One example of this was the discovery and application of nuclear magnetic resonance (NMR). In the late 1940s Bloch and Purcell received the Nobel prize for detecting nuclear magnetism in bulk matter. Chemists rapidly began using NMR to study molecular structure, and by the 1960s, the necessary implementation had become so widely available and so inexpensive that almost every research chemist in the United States could use the technique. The development of superconducting magnets, computerized instrumentation, and Fourier Transform techniques enhanced the sensitivity of NMR. Meanwhile, imaging techniques developed during the 1970s led to the ability to analyze proton density in biological systems, which in the 1980s forms the basis of the current experimental use of NMR in the detection of human cancer, clogged arteries, and other disease states.

Most discoveries in basic science and their subsequent development are taken for granted and never become scientific issues. Such was the case with NMR. But new techniques sometimes produce data that are difficult to deal with in the arena of public policy. This is particularly true when advances in one field of science proceed more rapidly than those in a companion field, for example, the advances made in the analysis of chemicals in the environment.

Although extremely sensitive techniques are available now, there is potential for analysts to go far beyond today's measurement capabilities. One liter of alcohol uniformly distributed in the earth's vast supply of water corresponds to about 10^{-18} ppm. That is probably twelve orders of magnitude below the detection limits of even our most sensitive analytical instruments. However, if ethanol were stable and did not decompose, there would be about 2,500 molecules of alcohol in each liter of water sampled from the earth's supply. We cannot detect 2,500 molecules today, but we eventually may, and we will then discover not only ethanol but many other chemicals as well. The issue is here today and it will become more intense in the future: what is the significance of finding a material, even one responsible for human disease when consumed in large quantities, at very low concentrations in our environment? Toxicologists have dealt with this problem for years, but in the arena of public policy it is and will continue to be a significant issue.

A report on the human health effects of hazardous chemical exposures, assembled by the National Academy of Sciences at the request of Dr. George A. Keyworth, identified those research areas that were likely to return the highest scientific dividends as a result of incremental federal investments in the 1984 fiscal year.[1] The panel identified six areas, also identified by the American Industrial Health Council, as likely to contribute valuable information to issues of concern in regulatory programs.

—Research to improve the basis for dose and interspecies extrapolations to humans.

—Research into prediction of the effects of multiple chemical exposures.

—Improvement in the approaches to the determination of the reproductive and developmental effects of chemicals.

—Development of cellular and molecular markers of exposure to chemicals and markers of preclinical effects.

—Development and evaluation of techniques to categorize chemical carcinogens on the basis of modes of action.

—Expanded use of existing federal data-collection activities for assessing the effects on human health of various environmental pollutants and work-place hazards.

Research in these areas is important because the results will have an effect on national regulatory policies for producing, distributing, and using hazardous materials. Government regulations affect the ability of U.S. industry to supply needs and to do so competitively in the world market. Everyone seems to agree that it is desirable to use the best scientific understanding available in regulatory programs, but with rapid technological changes and increasing specialization it is difficult to determine what constitutes "the best scientific understanding."

Dr. Arnold L. Brown, dean of the medical school at the University of Wisconsin, has spoken about one of the areas in which further research is needed—the development of cellular and molecular markers of exposure to chemicals: "The common thread running through all of toxicological research is the definition of biological endpoints. In times past our techniques to identify such endpoints were relatively crude and the markers were, therefore, fairly obvious. We looked for such things as cancer, gross neurological signs, weight loss, anemia, hemorrhage, hair loss, or grossly visible organ lesions or changes that lit up under standard light microscopy. Now the harbingers of a biological effect are signalled by such endpoints as a frameshift or point

1. *Report of the Research Briefing Panel on Human Health Effects of Hazardous Chemicals* (National Academy Press, 1983).

mutation, an increase in alphafetoprotein, DNA repair, changes in the concentrations of an isoenzyme, or a computer derived, and subtle, alteration in an electroencephalogram. Thus, by the use of new concepts and new methods, the emphasis has shifted from the diagnosis of overt disease to the identification of changes that are believed to anticipate such diseases."[2]

I am encouraged and excited by the advances being made in identifying biological markers for disease as they may eventually help to prevent such diseases. Yet there are clouds on the horizon, at least from the perspective of public policy. William D. Carey, executive director of the American Association for the Advancement of Science, said the American public has "science anxiety," which he defined as a "state of nerves related to the multiple dilemmas associated with the siting of nuclear power plants, the disposal of radioactive and toxic wastes, the mysterious goings-on in genetic engineering, the failures of diplomacy in reaching verifiable strategic arms control agreements, repeated scares about drug and pesticide safety, contradictory findings about cancer-producing elements in food processing and packaging, and ill-advised pronouncements on all sorts of scientific matters by scientists with name-recognition who venture outside their fields of expertise."[3]

Combine this science anxiety with the increasing degree of scientific specialization and the technological illiteracy that inevitably results for most of us, and one begins to comprehend the dimensions of the dilemma. Newspaper reports about changes in biological markers, which may or may not be related to disease but which are produced by exposing laboratory animals or man to a chemical substance with an exotic-sounding name, may well produce an immediate outcry for action. Congress, being politically astute but often baffled by scientific complexity and uncertainty, is likely to respond.

One contentious issue is chemical carcinogenicity. During the past decade we have poured massive federal, industrial, and academic research efforts into studies of carcinogenic agents. The studies have gone beyond the simplistic bioassay to studies of pharmacokinetics, metabolism, genetic alteration, DNA binding and repair, epidemiology, and exposure assessments. The research

2. Arnold L. Brown, "The Frontiers of Toxicology," paper prepared for the 1982 annual meeting of the American Industrial Health Council, Washington, D.C., November 29, 1982.

3. William D. Carey, paper prepared for the 1982 annual meeting of the Society of Environmental Toxicology and Chemistry.

has produced much new knowledge and it needs to continue. Yet we have a regulatory program that focuses almost exclusively on a simplistic yes-or-no classification system for carcinogenic agents and pays little regard to much of the data that are available. Public policy is highly variable on this point; some laws ban carcinogenic agents, others require an ample margin of safety, and still others mandate a balancing of risks and benefits. The interrelatedness of policy, its implementation, and the understanding of scientific principles has never been clearer.

Some of the newer issues concerning environmental pollutants deal with acid rain and the greenhouse effect mediated by pollutants. Similarly there is concern for the reproductive and neurological effects of pollutants on human health. Each issue has its own peculiar set of nuances, but the basic needs that must be filled by the scientific community are the same: the development and periodic updating of a scientific consensus, the clear articulation of that consensus, and finally the effective incorporation of scientific fact and understanding into legislative and regulatory programs. Although what is required seems obvious, mechanisms for developing and communicating in a timely fashion scientific positions on issues of national concern need to be established and made effective.

I feel a sense of urgency about all this. There is no time like the present to better incorporate science into public policies dealing with environmental risk. Environmental laws frequently come up for review, and changes can be made. The recent discussion of changes in toxic tort laws further highlights the important role science must play in public policy. We need to direct some of the creativity shown by our scientists toward institutional changes that might better use in public policy those scientific developments relating to environmental risk.

Five possible steps to achieve this goal come to mind. First, incentives should be provided for top scientists to get involved in regulatory programs. This means that the results of scientific analyses of regulatory proposals need to be given prominence. It also means laws need to be written in a manner that demands the use of scientific analysis and provides the flexibility needed for the analysis to be used.

Second, social decisions that go beyond objective scientific analysis should be clearly identified, so the public can be aware of the subjective decisions made for them by their elected officials.

Third, the peer-review system for scientific contributions to regulatory decisions should be strengthened.

Fourth, outside scientists intimately familiar with recent developments should be brought into the regulatory process at an early stage to ensure the incorporation of up-to-date and accurate scientific data.

Fifth, we need to learn to communicate more effectively with the general public on issues relating to the effect of chemicals on human health. Ultimately the political process is driven by public opinion, so to effectively deal with scientific issues in public policy, an informed public is a necessity.

Scientists have often ignored policy issues. Policymakers have often chosen to avoid scientific complexity. There may be room elsewhere for this type of specialization but not in the realm of public health policy. The issues and the science that underlies them must be brought together so that our course of action will be in the best interest of all.

The Clean Air Act: An Update

GILBERT S. OMENN

SENATOR Pete Domenici, a member of the Senate Committee on Environmental and Public Works, recently wrote:

> The Clean Air Act is stagnating—politically, conceptually and environmentally. The 1982 Congressional deliberations on the Clean Air Act generated a political stalemate and with only isolated exceptions the participants spent their time refighting a law unequipped to meet the challenges of the 80s. This political and intellectual stalemate has been accompanied by a slowdown in the rate of environmental progress which began in the late 1970s. Today, more than 40 million Americans still breathe air officially designated as "unhealthy" for at least one pollutant. Furthermore, the regulatory linchpin of the Clean Air Act, the State Implementation Plans (SIPs), has become a curse to all concerned.[1]

In the first Brookings Institution–American Industrial Health Council Symposium, held in the chamber of the House Committee on Science and Technology in July 1981, and subsequently in a monograph I coauthored with Lester Lave,[2] I identified the scientific and technical challenges we face in assessing the effects of pollutants on health, in revising and improving national ambient air-quality standards, in monitoring air quality, and in devising cost-effective and workable emissions-control strategies for both existing and new sources of air pollution. Some solutions to these problems required changes in the law; others necessitated changes in regulations or agency policy. Lave and I concluded that there is considerable potential for a more efficient and effective implementation of the Clean Air Act, whose goals are so widely supported by the American people. We do not face a zero-sum game. Much still remains to be done to convert the strong public sentiment for cleaner air into sound standard setting, meaningful monitoring, and effective enforcement.

1. Peter Domenici, "Emissions Trading: The Subtle Heresy," *Environmental Forum*, vol. 1 (December 1982), p. 24.
2. Lester B. Lave and Gilbert S. Omenn, *Clearing the Air: Reforming the Clean Air Act* (Brookings Institution, 1981).

What is the current status of the Clean Air Act? As 1983 commences, the situation is truly discouraging. Neither consensus nor compromise has emerged within Congress. The Reagan administration has had many false starts and has failed even to gain a foothold in the debates. No new standards have been promulgated by the EPA, and none have been revised. Environmentalists are frustrated that no progress has been made on hazardous pollutants and that so little has been learned about acid precipitation and what can be done about it. Business and industry are dissatisfied because so little movement has taken place in dealing with state implementation plans, in streamlining the cumbersome regulations that prevent significant deterioration in areas that meet national ambient air-quality standards, or in turning economic incentives and emissions-trading mechanisms into effective plans for emissions control. Business desperately needs consistent regulatory policy, not uncertain, changing EPA views. Finally consumers need assurance that expensive pollution-control equipment actually functions to specifications.

Is there any good news at all? Not much. Right now six congressional subcommittees are taking aim at the EPA. States are suing to avoid the sanctions mandated by the Clean Air Act for regions not in attainment of clean air standards as of December 31, 1982. States in many areas of the country are dropping inspection and maintenance programs for mobile sources of pollution. Nevertheless, there is progress on several fronts, and I remain optimistic for the longer term.

First, there is growing interest in relevant studies and real data on the health effects of specific pollutants. For example, adults and adolescents with asthma or other lung diseases have been shown to be more susceptible to sulfur dioxide than nonasthmatics.[3] Previously standards were set to protect such people based only on presumptions of higher susceptibility.

There is also some movement among researchers to examine the effects of criteria pollutants at concentrations relevant for regulatory decisions. In the past, animal and clinical exposure studies used such high concentrations of suspect chemicals that little direct information could be gained for the difficult decisions about choosing particular levels for air-quality standards. The Health Effects Institute, a consortium of manufacturers joined with the EPA to provide funding for peer-reviewed research, is

3. Jane Q. Koenig, William E. Pierson, Martha Horike, and Robert Frank, "A Comparison of the Pulmonary Effects of 0.5 ppm versus 1.0 ppm Sulfur Dioxide plus Sodium Chloride Droplets in Asthmatic Adolescents," *Journal of Toxicology and Environmental Health*, vol. 11 (1983), pp. 129–39.

making its initial round of grants for research into its special area of interest: the effects of diesel exhaust. A wide range of proposals were received from leading research centers.

Second, there is growing recognition that some changes are overdue in regard to ambient air-quality standards. The total-suspended-particulate standard has long been criticized for its overrepresentation of particles (by mass) that cannot be inhaled into the deep passages of the lung. Unfortunately, the proposed ranges for primary and secondary inhalable particulates in the new standard have been interpreted as equivalent to a relaxation of the total-suspended-particulates standard.[4] I believe that the standards for inhalable particles and for sulfur compounds should be tightened, while those for ozone might justifiably be relaxed. The evidence on the susceptibility of asthmatics has fueled demand for a short-term standard for sulfur dioxide.[5] Still to be addressed is the contention of Lave and Seskin that acid sulfates may be the most harmful of the criteria pollutants in the air, accounting for excess mortality in susceptible persons.[6] In contrast, ozone seems to cause only acute and transient effects (though long-term effects have not been well studied). There should be much more attention paid to the other important parameter of the national ambient air-quality standard, the number of exceedances permitted per year.

Increasing the number of exceedances permitted is statistically equivalent to relaxing the standard to a higher value with one exceedance per year; however, the same pseudothreshold value would be retained and the transient nature of the health effects would be acknowledged. The contrast between sulfates and ozone illustrates the importance of specifying and eventually comparing the nature and seriousness of adverse health effects caused by different kinds of pollutants rather than regulating each pollutant with equal vigor and disregarding the health gains to be achieved.

A far more disconcerting difference has emerged in the approach to hazardous pollutants as compared with criteria pollutants. The EPA's long-awaited airborne-carcinogens policy, announced in 1979,[7] challenged the clear congressional requirement in section

4. Bette Hileman, "Particulate Matter: The Inhalable Variety," *Environmental Science and Technology*, vol. 15 (September 1981), pp. 983–86.

5. Homer Boushey, "Asthma, Sulfur Dioxide, and the Clean Air Act," *Western Journal of Medicine*, vol. 136 (February 1982), pp. 129–35.

6. See Lester B. Lave and Eugene Seskin, *Air Pollution and Human Disease* (Johns Hopkins University Press, 1977).

7. Environmental Protection Agency, "National Emissions Standards for Hazardous Air Pollutants: Policy and Procedures for Identifying, Assessing, and Regulating Airborne Substances Posing a Risk of Cancer," *Federal Register*, vol. 44 (October 10, 1979), p. 58642.

112 of the Clean Air Act that particularly hazardous pollutants (such as known carcinogens) be regulated to zero-risk levels and that even then there be an ample margin of safety. Most environmental groups have been critical of the EPA for its slow pace in generating section 112 standards. David Hawkins, the former head of the air program, said that the EPA suffered from "paralysis by analysis" in its attempts to initiate actions against the most potentially hazardous pollutants. The 1979 policy required the public to accept "remaining risks" and required industry only to apply the best available control technology. This approach—specifying the nature of the risks and analyzing the kinds of effects and the likely number of people to be affected at each level of exposure—allows for a rational assessment of acceptable remaining risks in light of the feasibility of compliance with alternative standards. So far as I can ascertain, the bill that was approved 15–1 in the Senate Committee on Environment and Public Works to reauthorize the Clean Air Act failed to acknowledge this important shift by the EPA toward a potentially workable approach for hazardous pollutants.

The problem of thresholds is not limited to carcinogens. Individual differences in sensitivity and variable routes of exposures make it difficult to demonstrate a noneffect or threshold level for other pollutants. But if no threshold level can be identified, how can a margin of safety be subtracted?

Third, I believe that the EPA is continuing to make progress on the siting and quality control of air-quality monitors.[8] Whether these efforts will be sustained in the face of budget reductions by the Reagan administration is uncertain. If monitoring is irregular or readily manipulated, the whole enforcement strategy is jeopardized.

Fourth, there is growing recognition that the EPA must relinquish at least some aspects of its "command and control" approach to emissions regulation. More responsibility must be delegated to the states for decisions about point sources, once an overall state implementation plan has been approved. At present it is often something of a mystery whether or not such a plan has been approved and in what form. Each year there are more advocates for economic incentives: bubble policies, offsets for nonattainment regions, or emissions-reduction credits (as urged by Senator Domenici), and so on. Richard A. Liroff has published a particularly instructive analysis and review of offset policies and

8. Based on a personal communication with Walter Barber, 1982.

their implementation with banking arrangements.[9] Much work must be done to evaluate these approaches, and special efforts will be required to avoid manipulation. Emissions reductions must be real, not nominal, and industry must have some protection against being penalized for innovative emissions-control technologies.

Finally, the polls show strong support for the goals of the Clean Air Act. There is majority support for inspection and maintenance programs for automobiles in the states that have such programs, and there appears to be similar support in other states that need such programs to reach attainment status.[10] The willingness of the general public to actually participate in steps that help to reduce emissions is far more impressive than simple expressions of desire for clean air. A tougher test of public responsiveness will come when taxpayers are asked to help to underwrite the costs of reducing sulfur- and nitrogen-containing emissions from utilities, possibly by removing the tall stacks that solved the local air pollution problem, or by applying other technologies to reduce the risk of acid rain hundreds or thousands of miles away!

The air we breathe is a critical resource and a crucial environmental factor in our health. We must pursue many avenues for improvement in the Clean Air Act to achieve our clean air goals.

9. Richard A. Liroff, *Air Pollution Offsets: Trading, Selling, and Banking* (Washington, D.C.: Conservation Foundation, 1980).

10. Michael Walsh, *Environmental Forum* (August 1982), pp. 14–19.

Etiological Factors in Human Cancer

JOHN HIGGINSON

I BELIEVE that there are now enough data to permit rational public health approaches to some of the problems of cancer prevention in humans. Recent reviews on the etiology of cancer in the United States and other industrialized countries are in general agreement on the main etiological categories.[1] These and other reports have emphasized the importance of life-style factors in human cancer causation, though the relative role of individual components remains uncertain.

Cancer patterns in North America and Europe today are similar to those observed at the turn of the century. This indicates that the causal agents of many cancers must have been present for a considerable period. It may also mean that no obvious new cancer epidemic may be attributed to generalized environmental pollution or other new factors.[2] There are, however, some notable exceptions.

Tobacco- and alcohol-related cancers have shown a marked increase in both industrialized and nonindustrialized countries, especially since World War II. The rise in esophageal cancer in blacks is of particular concern in the United States. There has been a marked fall in stomach cancer since the 1930s in the United States, Western Europe, and, more recently, Japan. The relatively slight changes in the incidence of cancer at other sites can largely be explained by recent changes in diagnostic criteria, life styles, and so forth, rather than by new carcinogenic agents. On the occupational side, the incidence of asbestos-related occupational cancers may be reaching a plateau. On the other hand, an epidemic of several hundred cases of Kaposi's sarcoma has occurred in the

---

1. Richard Doll and Richard Peto, "The Avoidable Causes of Cancer," *OUP* (New York, 1981); E. L. Wynder and G. B. Gori, "Contribution of the Environment to Cancer Incidence: An Epidemiological Exercise," *Journal of National Cancer Institute*, vol. 58 (1977), p. 825; and John Higginson and C. S. Muir, "Environmental Carcinogenesis: Misconceptions and Limitations to Cancer Control," *Journal of National Cancer Institute*, vol. 63 (1979), p. 1291.

2. Doll and Peto, "Avoidable Causes."

United States; this is believed to have been caused by a new type of viral infection in homosexual adults. These and other trends have important implications for public health strategies that cannot be discussed here.

It is unfortunate that the number of cancer studies from nonindustrialized or semi-industrialized states is small, since such studies would be of great help in evaluating the effect on health of factors associated with modern societies. In countries adopting a Western life style, patterns in cancer and other diseases (especially heart disease) resemble those seen in North America and Europe. In Japan and Singapore significant differences remain, though studies on Japanese migrants to the United States suggest that important changes may occur during the next two decades.

Although our general views on cancer risk factors have not changed significantly in recent years, there have been interesting developments in basic and epidemiological research that are relevant to public policy.

Carcinogens and carcinogenic mechanisms

The term "carcinogen" can be applied to any agent that induces or tends to induce cancer in man or animals irrespective of mechanism.[3] Some modulating agents are tumor promoters and may enhance tumor formation; other agents may inhibit carcinogenesis. There is no consensus on action mechanisms of many such agents, and this makes for a lack of terminological clarity. I believe that it is better to use the term "carcinogenic agent" or "stimulus" to describe any agent, risk factor, or defined chemical that is associated with an increase in cancer in humans. Thus the term could include both initiators, which cause significant damage to genetic material (vinyl chloride, for example), and promoters, which are not believed to affect DNA directly (hormones, for example).

In contrast, the large group of nonspecific dietary factors (unsaturated fats, insufficient dietary fiber, and the like) or behavioral habits (age at pregnancy) could be described as risk factors but not as carcinogens. The significance of each risk factor should be considered on an ad hoc basis in terms of mechanism and preventive strategy. There are many gray zones in which modulating factors will be difficult to evaluate, but they must be considered in regulatory action. That different carcinogenic stimuli

3. Committee of the Health Council, Ministry of Health and Environmental Protection, *The Evaluation of the Carcinogenicity of Chemical Substances* (The Hague: Government Printing Office, 1980).

operate through a range of mechanisms may have significant implications for the regulation of carcinogens, a view accepted by the Dutch government[4] but few others.

Life style

Apart from such habits as smoking and drinking, there remains considerable uncertainty as to the specific effects of many life-style factors. Although there is widespread agreement that diet and nutrition represent the most important components of life style and have a significant effect on cancer patterns,[5] the mechanisms involved are still a matter for research and the data are not sufficient to permit definitive conclusions about the role of many individual nutrients.

Most people accept the fact that low fiber and excess-fat intake are important in cancer, but studies on different kinds of cancer (such as breast, large bowel, and prostate) among Mormons, Seventh Day Adventists, vegetarian and nonvegetarian nuns, Finns versus Danes, migrants, and so on, do not suggest a simple causal relationship between cancer and fat consumption. It is far from established that a simple reduction of dietary fat alone will be effective in reducing the incidence of breast, prostate, or intestinal cancer, especially if such dietary reductions commence only in adult life.

An examination of the National Research Council's review of dietary factors and cancer shows many inconsistencies in epidemiological observations. Unfortunately, the NRC report did not address itself to the issue of dietary changes early in life, though there is considerable data indicating that many dietary factors have their greatest influence at that time. Even though marked changes have taken place in the American diet over the last twenty years, there is no evidence that these have had an effect on cancer patterns, though studies of migrants suggest some variations and changes should have been observed. Some recent changes in the incidence of breast cancer can be attributed to modifications in reproductive habits rather than to diet; for the moment the question remains open.

While the NRC report confirmed earlier studies that there was little evidence that the multiplicity of carcinogens or mutagens in food was important in human cancer, it reinforced the view that diet is an important part of life style and that its role will probably be explained within the concept of multistage carcinogenesis.

4. Ibid.

5. National Research Council, Assembly on Life Sciences, Committee on Diet, Nutrition, and Cancer, *Diet, Nutrition, and Cancer* (Washington, D.C.: NRC, 1982).

Multistage carcinogenesis

Although the concept of multistage carcinogenesis was recognized over forty years ago, only recently has its significance to preventive strategies become widely recognized. The way in which normal cells are transformed into cancer cells is not clear. Recent developments suggest a role for oncogenes, genes that are not normally expressed but whose expression is required for cancer to develop. The current data still leave open the question of how such genes might be triggered.

Rapid-screening tests for carcinogenic potential (for example, the Ames test) are widely used, but few believe that they do any more than show a substance's carcinogenic potential. The tests cannot be used to prove carcinogenicity or potency in man.[6] The same problem holds for animal models. No systematic program has been developed to study how the effects of known human carcinogens might be extrapolated more accurately from animal or other models. In only a few cases have comparative metabolic studies of different species been used for the extrapolation calculations. If there is no adequate method available to extrapolate for known human carcinogens, what is the value of assigning numerical risk values to potential carcinogens? At most, such values can provide only a certain degree of comfort rather than scientific security, though that may be of some value in the practical aspects of risk assessment.

Occupational cancer

Despite intense efforts by epidemiologists, no major new occupational carcinogens have been identified in humans in the last ten years. Nonetheless the problem of occupational cancer remains a great concern, and it would not be surprising if new carcinogenic hazards were identified in the work place in the future. Because of improved engineering practices and the changing nature of the U.S. work force, however, it is possible that worker exposure to the traditional chemical carcinogens will decrease at least in large industries. The main concern will then be for the consumer or for small workshops, where careless practices are more likely to occur.

There continues to be concern about the escape of industrial carcinogens like asbestos into the general environment. But Doll and Peto have shown that there is little evidence that ambient pollution by classical carcinogens has had a significant effect on cancer patterns in industrialized states.[7] This in no way obviates

6. International Agency for Research on Cancer, *IARC Monographs on the Evaluation of the Carcinogenic Risk of Chemicals to Humans*, vols. 1–29 (Lyon, France: IARC, 1982).

7. Doll and Peto, "Avoidable Causes."

the need to evaluate on a systematic basis the health and ecological effects of suspected carcinogens. Occupational studies may provide a solid scientific base on which to evaluate the probable effects in humans of suspect chemicals at low doses, as those escaping from hazardous waste deposits. There is also concern about exposure to new chemical carcinogens in new and untested compounds. It is my opinion that the number of such chemicals is less than is generally believed and that few really new chemicals have entered the work place in recent years. Most are merely new formulations or modifications of older chemicals.

The effect of socioeconomic factors on occupational cancer is now receiving greater attention.[8] Although there have been few comparable studies in the United States, studies in the United Kingdom have estimated that nearly 90 percent of the differences in occupational cancers are due to socioeconomic factors. In some large concerns—DuPont, for example—the overall incidence of cancer is 10 to 20 percent below the average for the United States as a whole;[9] this cannot be ascribed solely to the classical healthy worker effect. From the viewpoint of public health strategy, it would appear equally important to determine why the general population has a higher rate of cancer, clearly an enormous problem, than to concentrate only on the problems of work-place exposure.

Cancer phobia   In the past, cancer phobia, or excessive fear of cancer, was a problem in clinical medicine. A great accomplishment of the American Cancer Society in the 1960s was to reduce such fear by bringing the facts before the public. But during the last decade, a new form of mass cancer phobia has become widespread in the United States. This fear relates to the possible development of cancer because of community exposure to carcinogens in low doses from a wide variety of sources such as hazardous waste deposits, air pollutants, and food additives. Such fears can lead to psychosomatic illness and ill health.[10] At a time when life expectancy has never been higher and when the quality of life in old age is considerably improved, it may be asked whether this

8. Office of Population Consensus and Surveys, *Occupational Mortality; the Registrar General's Decennial Supplement for England and Wales,* series DS, no. 1 (London: Her Majesty's Stationery Office, 1970–72).

9. S. Pell, M. T. O'Berg, and B. W. Karrh, "Cancer Epidemiologic Surveillance in the DuPont Company," *Journal of Occupational Medicine,* vol. 20 (1978), p. 725.

10. "Assessment of Health Effects at Chemical Disposal Sites," in W. W. Lawrence, ed., *Life Sciences and Public Policy Programs* (Rockefeller University, 1981).

generalized fear of cancer is either good or justifiable. Nevertheless, people appear to make fear of cancer paramount and to forget that there are many other illnesses as well.

So far this cancer phobia does not appear to have affected other industrialized nations (with the possible exception of Canada) to the same extent as the United States. In my opinion, this fear is not based on an accurate appreciation of the causes of human cancer either now or in the future; there is thus a large gap between the reality and public perception. This gap is widened by a distrust of public officials and by poorly balanced articles in the media. From a medical point of view, it is unethical to make people afraid unless a benefit can be demonstrated at the individual level. There is need to strengthen the evaluation process and to rigorously analyze and publicize the results.

Future Directions for Science and Policy

WILLIAM W. LOWRANCE

SCIENCE can be applied much more effectively to regulatory decisionmaking if we develop a number of policy goals.

First, unglamorous though the work may be, we must press to establish more solid health-data baselines upon which to evaluate health risks. Every time we need to assess the risks of a toxic waste dump, an Agent Orange, a Three Mile Island, or some other health hazard, we find ourselves without knowledge of "normal" health status.

Reproductive health is one example. We do not know nearly enough about spontaneous abortion; we only know, from a few isolated in-depth case reviews, that a staggeringly large percentage of pregnancies (probably over 30 percent) are terminated spontaneously. We know too little about premature and low-birth-weight births, infectious infant diseases, malnutrition, and birth defects, since fully reliable statistics are not developed for such problems (except for birthweight). Nor do we know enough about sperm counts, morphology, motility, or enzymology. Yet in public health emergencies, investigators probe all these indexes. If one does not know individuals' count histories or fluctuations, or the average and variation in the male population in general, how can one make any inferences either for the individuals or for the population? Infertility, twin ratios, gender ratios, and other indexes are no better understood. We do not know the baseline status for most communities, the mechanisms through which harm occurs, or even what would constitute appropriate "control" populations for comparison.

The same analytic limitations afflict most other health investigations, such as chromosome studies, cirrhosis, neurotoxicology studies, and assays of blood markers. What is clear is that the more we search for impairments in health, or at least for abnormalities in corporal composition or performance, the more abnormalities and impairments we will find.

50

The federal agencies concerned with basic health research, especially the National Institutes of Health, the National Institute of Mental Health, and the National Center for Health Statistics, should be supported in building these data bases—both through their own long-term allocations and by pass-through grants from regulatory agencies.

Second, we must develop the means for critiquing major assessory studies and reports. Reports like the Doll and Peto survey of the causes of cancer, the Lave and Omenn report on the Clean Air Act, the Interagency Regulatory Liaison Group guidelines on carcinogen assessment, and the Benbrook report on the regulation of pesticides tend to serve as benchmarks.[1] Thus it is crucial that they be critiqued broadly and carefully. I have urged *Science* magazine to commission reviews of such studies. Federal advisory committees also could perform this function, as could the National Academy of Sciences and the American Association for the Advancement of Science. Many other avenues of review are available; all should be encouraged.

Third, we must develop ways to accommodate new scientific understanding into regulations. Each regulatory program should try to foster consistency and to specify the criteria by which it makes rulings, but at the same time it must remain open, not just to new findings about particular regulated items but also to revisions in fundamental scientific-judgmental understanding. This is not easy. Often it requires elaborate deliberations separate from case-specific rulemaking. I agree with the spirit of the recommendation made by the recent National Research Council report on risk assessment, which urges the establishment of a high-level committee to scrutinize generic scientific aspects of regulations.[2] Ultimately, however, each agency, in conjunction with its advisers and Congress, must adopt its own standards.

Fourth, we must work toward anticipating and accommodating

---

1. Richard Doll and Richard Peto, *The Causes of Cancer* (Oxford and New York: Oxford University Press, 1981); Lester B. Lave and Gilbert S. Omenn, *Clearing the Air: Reforming the Clean Air Act* (Brookings Institution, 1981); U.S. Interagency Regulatory Liaison Group, Work Group on Risk Assessment, "Scientific Bases for Identification of Potential Carcinogens and Estimation of Risks," *Journal of the National Cancer Institute,* vol. 63 (1979), pp. 241–68; and Department of Operations, Research, and Foreign Agriculture Subcommittee of the House Committee on Agriculture, "Regulatory Procedures and Public Health Issues in the EPA's Office of Pesticide Programs," draft report, December 1982.

2. National Research Council, Committee on the Institutional Means for Assessment of Risks to Public Health, *Risk Assessment in the Federal Government: Managing the Process* (Washington, D.C.: National Academy Press, 1983).

demographic and hazard-apprehension changes. As the American population ages and the work force becomes more heterogeneous, morbidity and mortality patterns will change. Concern will increase not just about heart disease and cancer but about a variety of reproductive, genetic, immunological, and behavioral debilitations. The recent lobbying to establish a separate National Arthritis Institute within the National Institutes of Health is a manifestation of this trend.

It is important that we continue to evaluate on a comparative basis the different causes of infant mortality, occupational illness, longevity erosion, and other such matters. Sets within which we might compare the varying degrees of risk include physical agents having narrowly definable effects, societal functions, geographic areas, different industries or product classes, and contributions to specified illnesses or to mortality. Such analyses could indicate priority-risk candidates for research, reduction of exposure to particular products, redistribution of workers, or compensation. Priority might, for instance, be given to the biggest contributors to illness, discomfort, or disability (rheumatism, hearing impairment?); the problems most tractable or cost-effective of solution (lessening the number of infant fatalities in automobile accidents by requiring child restraints?); or the most unjust risks (brown lung disease?). These analyses must be conducted with sophistication: superficial comparisons are worse than useless.

We should promote industrial and government programs that pursue basic research and monitoring of such understudied problems as reproductive and genetic hazards, psychological stress (especially the kind associated with the difficulties at Love Canal and Three Mile Island), and immunological hazards.

Evaluation admittedly is complicated by the continual development and discovery of new potential hazards—production-scale handling of recombinant DNA, video display screens, interferon, and so on—even though these accompany exciting benefits.

Fifth, we must continue to press the ultimate issue of what levels of risk are judged "reasonable," "acceptable," or "tolerable," for what degrees of benefit. These terms gain operational definition only as regulatory decisions are made. Even then their meanings often cannot be inferred until the implicit valuation is translated into explicit valuation (as reflected, for instance, in court awards or regulatory cost assessments). The Nuclear Regulatory Commission's recently promulgated reactor safety goals are a powerful test case, as are the pesticide residue tolerances set by the EPA in conjunction with the FDA and the Department of Agriculture.

The Occupational Safety and Health Administration's ruling on benzene, negated by a 1980 Supreme Court ruling, exemplified how hard it is to decide whether the marginal gains in health protection are worth the economic costs incurred.

Sixth, we must prepare to confront the difficult issue of protective discrimination. Discrimination need not be a pejorative term. We have always selected people differentially for jobs, military tasks, and other functions. Genetic screening as a condition for employment raises the question of discrimination, as does the debate over how restrictive to make the Clean Air Act in order to protect people who suffer from asthma and emphysema. Allergies are common and staggeringly diverse. As we learn more about immunology and other basic characteristics of people, these diversities and complexities will increase.

Almost certainly we will want to discriminate between the older and the younger, the strong-backed and the weak-framed, the overweight stroke-prone and the cardiac robust, the child-bearing and those past childbearing. But clearly "individuation" of food and pharmaceutical choice and differential treatment in areas such as employment will conflict squarely with equal opportunity and will challenge paternalistic policies. Facing these issues will not be easy, but we should confront them now before they become intractable.

I do not see a strong need for new laws or institutions, but I do see a definite need to make much better use of those that exist. Every regulatory agency has available informal and formal advisers, arrangements for supplemental external research, and access to other organizations offering help. The enabling legislation for most agencies is flexible enough to cover the issues they must address. Implementation is the problem.

We should try to draw insights from the wide range of experience we have accumulated in dealing with the emergencies over kepone, vinyl chloride, polychlorinated biphenyls, Love Canal, and toxic shock syndrome. We must learn to deal with long-term issues like black-lung disease and asbestos; with personally contentious issues such as asbestos in hair driers, diethylstilbestrol (DES), and laetrile; and with such difficult-to-appraise issues as the safety of saccharin, occupational exposure to benzene, and polio vaccination. Some detailed case studies have been performed, but more need to be made, published, and subjected to organized, critical review.

But surely what is most important is to encourage and support competent people of goodwill in all these difficult endeavors.

Risk Analysis at the Office of Technology Assessment

JOHN H. GIBBONS

IN THINKING ABOUT the subject of risk taking and risk analysis, I was reminded of the years I spent at Oak Ridge National Laboratory. The community of Oak Ridge lies along a ridge that overlooks the escarpment of the Cumberland Mountains, the western edge of the great East Tennessee Valley. From atop that ridge, one can see many things: coal strip mines slowly but inexorably taking the tops off the western horizon, sunsets made brilliant by the exhaust of a coal-fired plant, rising clouds of water vapor from the cooling towers of the gaseous diffusion plant that enriches uranium for weapons and nuclear power production, and nuclear reactors a few miles away.

Confrontation of the manifestations of energy technology in a setting of splendid beauty made a deep and lasting impression on me: how far can human ingenuity, through technology, go in terms of enabling us to enjoy the benefits of technology while enduring minimum negative effects of technology? It did not take much analysis to quantitatively affirm the observation made earlier by Ralph Waldo Emerson, "Nature never gives anything to anyone; everything is sold at a price. It is only in the ideals of abstraction that choice comes without consequences."

I was also reminded of a cartoon in *Scientific American* that showed a woman seated at a lunch counter, contemplating a menu posted on the wall. One column in the menu listed hamburgers, cheeseburgers, and various other items. Next to it were two more columns describing the risks and benefits of each selection. I think many in American society came to that lunch counter in the 1970s and asked about those two columns, wanting to know not just about the imposed risks they faced but also about the risks they might somehow control in their personal lives. Many studies done in the 1970s pointed out the enormous influence one's life style has on so-called risks.

One study that dealt comprehensively with the risks associated with energy production and use was a report by the Committee on Nuclear and Alternative Energy Systems. This analysis, with which I was involved, was conducted under the auspices of the National Academy of Sciences, and it helped to clarify the types and magnitudes of energy-related risks. In doing so, the report provided an information base for more informed economic and energy-policy debates.

Later, the National Coal Policy Project provided me with another important learning experience—the value of gathering all stakeholders around the same table so that they might learn to communicate effectively about the highly charged issues surrounding coal despite their strong differences in orientation. We found that by using the process of cooperative dissent, people who were knowledgeable about their specialties but very different in their concerns about coal could stay problem-focused and could learn to adjudicate about coal—where it should be mined, how it should be used, what one should watch out for, and so on. The process worked so well that when Congress finally had to wrestle with problems in coal mining and combustion processes, as many as three-fourths of the issues that had been in dispute were already agreed on by the opposing sides in the debate. Our early work helped to raise the quality of the debate and to set the stage not only for legislative resolution of many of the issues but also for a wiser set of ultimate decisions. It seems to me that such procedures could play a key role in the development of public policy and in the resolution of complex and controversial socio-technical issues.

I believe that trying to fully separate scientific analysis from the rest of the decisionmaking process limits its value. The question is how we can develop a scientific basis for decisionmaking and at the same time incorporate the very real and important social issues involved.

Risk analysis does have its role, but it can sometimes be abused by people who are not that careful or skilled in its use. Some people can add up the strangest things to get a particular result, a truism illustrated by yet another cartoon in *Scientific American*: a driver looking out of his car window sees a sign saying "Entering Hillsville. Founded: 1802. Altitude: 620. Population: 3,700. Total: 6,122." The moral is that you have to be careful about how you add and be sure that the means justify the ends, not vice versa.

Studies at the Office of Technology Assessment

We use risk analysis at the congressional Office of Technology Assessment, where we are charged with the impossible—assessing the physical, biological, economic, social, and political aspects and effects of new technologies.

I believe the various studies OTA has done have helped to clarify options and to raise the quality of public debate. We have been deeply involved in studies on cancer risks, nuclear waste management, MX basing alternatives, atmospheric emissions (especially acid rain), and the effect of Agent Orange on Vietnam War veterans.

We at OTA are nearly finished with a major study on nonnuclear toxic and hazardous wastes, a subject that seems to be attracting more attention these days than in the past. We have become more forward-looking than retrospective in trying to understand the things that now are moving into the waste stream and in trying to develop processes that can help to reduce the toxic and hazardous nature of these materials. We have also been asked by the senators from New York to assist them in assessing whether state-of-the-art techniques are being used to monitor and control toxic wastes in Love Canal and in determining the degree of hazard still in the area and whether the rehabitability decision stands up under scrutiny.

We have been involved in a survey on the use of genetic screening methods in the work place. We are in the middle of a study of work-place hazards that should be finished in the fall, and we have just begun a study on ground-water contamination across the continental United States, including Alaska. I suspect that we may soon undertake some work on the issues of reproductive hazards and alternatives to animal testing. These are questions on which Congress is seriously seeking thoughtful advice.

We are also involved in another kind of risk analysis: studying the viability of our strategic command, control, communications, and intelligence systems. Although that issue is qualitatively different from the kinds of risk under discussion at this workshop, we apply the same procedures we use elsewhere: identifying and putting together the parties at interest, finding experts, going to work on the question, and then transmitting the results to Congress.

The commonality among the diverse kinds of risk analyses OTA undertakes is not in the analytical methods or kinds of experts we use. It is instead in our procedures. One key procedure is to identify at the outset the parties at interest in the debate and to make sure that all those parties are called to the same advisory table. This assures us that as OTA undertakes a project, opposing points of view are forcefully represented. Our panels assist us in identifying information, both completed and in process, and in assessing its validity. We do not want to make unwarranted findings or tilt in one direction or another.

We want our studies to be substantive, to provide the facts as well as they can be determined scientifically. But we will also venture technical judgments about things that are not secure in the hard facts. Ultimately, we attempt to guarantee that whatever is delivered to Congress and the public is fair, gives the members a chance to understand why experts differ—and they almost always do—and details options Congress has in dealing with the problems. The weight given that kind of study by an individual member or a committee is very great and I believe of enormously greater importance than a narrow technical analysis. If OTA simply did technical studies, ignoring related economic and social concerns, it would mean only that much more homework for the members and committees of Congress. Therefore I have some reservations about the notion that a newly constituted "science panel" would be that important an innovation in the policy process.

I want to repeat that it is very difficult, at least based on my experience at OTA, to cleanly separate scientific inputs from social concerns in decisionmaking. Most sociotechnical policy issues are too complicated to be easily separated, and it is not realistic to ask our elected representatives to somehow reintegrate the pieces themselves.

I have also observed that scientific discoveries can exacerbate the difficulties of policymaking. Someone once said to me, "You may think that technology assessment is going to help policy-makers by giving them a self-consistent way of exploring alternatives. Unfortunately, what it can do instead is tie their hands and seemingly limit the number of options available to them. Don't think that what you are doing is necessarily going to help."

As an example, consider the zero-threshold phenomena—risks that have no threshold for impact. A zero-threshold situation leaves the policymaker in a great quandary. As long as there is some threshold level below which there are no ill effects, social equity can be preserved. But if dose and effect have a zero–zero intercept, then the policymaker must talk about determining acceptable risk, which is far more difficult to deal with than no risk.

Unfortunately, a zero-zero intercept is going to be what the picture looks like more frequently than not. How do you solve that problem? One way would be to devise a perfect technology, and I think that that's what many hoped for a decade ago. Now it seems that almost everyone recognizes that there is no perfect technology or magic bullet, and that we must therefore devise alternative strategies. My former boss Al Weinberg said, "What we ought to do is get the doses down very low, so that you have fewer effects to deal with. Then let's figure out how to cure the effects when they do appear, so that those who are affected can be treated and cured." That strategy, faulty as it may appear, may be our best hope in the absence of perfect technologies.

There are other problems. Consider the issue of delayed response to dose. As a policymaker or regulator, you may wish you could ignore delayed effects; they certainly complicate matters. But they are real.

I think that rather than talking about absolute risks, one way to approach the standards-setting problem is to say, "How large is the imposed risk compared to the differences in individual life styles?" If I change my life style, might that have one hundred times more effect than whatever risk is being imposed on me? I believe this might be a possible approach to adjudicating questions of inevitable social risks.

We are obviously not headed into easier waters, though I think we are, as a society, getting more realistic about both the promises and the limits of technology. One difficulty can be attributed to what I call the "N-square problem," that is, the number of interactions between people goes up as a square of the number of people. With more activity and interaction between people, there is a need for greater regulation among ourselves. In times past you might have an argument with your upwind neighbor over the smoke from his fireplace; now we have smoke moving 500 or more miles—across state and international boundaries. There is a new degree of magnitude in the interaction between those who are producing pollutants and those who are feeling the effects. We face new challenges in developing a degree of equity in this more complex, interactive society.

Ultimately we have to move toward consensus; without consensus we cannot innovate as a society—we cannot try things out. I once heard the ironic tale of a man who had invented a marvelous brake for the skateboard but was unable to market it because of the potential cost of product liability suits. As a result there are probably a lot more broken legs and arms than there need be. We are a litigious society, and that tends to constrain us quite massively. I think we need to understand that not to risk also has its penalties—not to take chances can lead to a very uninteresting and, I believe, undesirable future.

Industrial Perspective on Regulating Carcinogens

MONTE C. THRODAHL

THE PUBLIC perceives that there is a cancer problem in the work place, in the air, in water, and in products and materials. This fear is translated into legislative-regulatory actions by no-fault, zero-risk mentalities and into litigation that is changing the nature of the required proof-of-harm.

There is confusion and misinformation as well as genuine concern about carcinogens. Some emotionally charged but insignificant—even erroneous—data have been fed to the public with the intent of supporting philosophical, emotional, or political dogmas. Retroactive wisdom is often expected of industry. It appears that the concept of "involuntary" exposure limits, tantamount to bans, provides convenient opportunities to attack corporations, an "any-stick-will-do" syndrome. The net result is that chemical producers and users are placed in an untenable position.

From the industrial perspective, carcinogen regulation requires initiative and responsibility on the part of both government and industry in obtaining first-quality data upon which to base regulations as well as for monitoring, auditing, and enforcing compliance. Industry should be consistent in its performance and should speak up for fair treatment by regulators and legislators.

For several years a number of chemical companies have assumed full responsibility for establishing their own standards for monitoring environmental risk. In so doing they have taken action in the seven areas I have outlined below.

Initiate: to preserve an attitude of initiative and a policy of responsibility for the industry's actions on a worldwide basis.

Analyze: to gather, analyze, and validate facts pertinent to chemical structure, bioassays, and the environment with state-of-the-art knowledge.

Audit: to continually monitor and audit industry's own actions in the manufacture, distribution, use, and ultimate disposal of chemicals to identify the hazardous possible sources and extent of exposure, and then to analyze these observations for significance or insignificance.

59

Enforce: to enforce all environmental, safety, and health regulations at all levels and scales of operations, and to communicate this enforcement to the appropriate regulatory agencies.

Learn and innovate: to continually modify (or eliminate) manufacturing processes should any significant new knowledge indicate the possibility of chronic adverse health effects on man; to support fundamental research on the role of chemicals in carcinogenesis; and where possible, to carry out original research to learn why certain carcinogenic effects may be observed in certain products.

Tell: to be honest about the discovery of real problems and their correction, and to communicate appropriate information about risks as well as safety practices to persons who may be exposed during the manufacture, transport, use, or disposal of chemicals; to interpret and feed back this information to management and to the public consistently; to point out inconsistencies in regulatory decisions about potential carcinogens.

Use science well: to emphasize that everything else about carcinogen regulation is subsidiary to the quality of science that is used as a basis for regulatory decisionmaking.

In recent years we have seen the wasted resources, misdirection, and public confusion that have resulted from a failure to apply good science to environmental regulation. The list of mistakes is too long to detail here, but most of us are familiar with the major instances: the Interagency Regulatory Liaison Group[1] document on the identification of carcinogens, the generic cancer policy proposed by the Occupational Safety and Health Administration in 1977, the Love Canal regulatory decisions by the EPA, and the nitrites-in-bacon decision.

Failure to properly apply science in these and other instances has created a crisis of confidence in our ability not only to deal with problems but also to identify them correctly. All the examples I have cited are based on unsound science or on invalidated data bases, particularly the refutation by the Thomas Committee of the health data used by the EPA at Love Canal.[2] The time to separate scientific definition from legal or social policymaking is

1. The Interagency Regulatory Liaison Group included several regulatory agencies, including the Food and Drug Administration, the Occupational Health and Safety Administration, the Environmental Protection Agency, and the Consumer Products Safety Commission.

2. "Report of the Panel to Review Scientific Studies and the Development of Public Policy on Problems Resulting from Hazardous Wastes." (The panel was created by executive order of the governor of New York on June 4, 1980, with Lewis Thomas, M.D., of the Memorial Sloan-Kettering Cancer Center, as chairman.)

long overdue. Scientific knowledge is often fragile and must be treated with respect, but lack of scientific knowledge is no excuse for making foolish decisions, just as ignorance of the law is not an allowable excuse for breaking it.

A basic distinction often misunderstood is that science defines perceived reality, whereas law decides codes of conduct. In making decisions, the law should make use of the best definitions available. This has long been the case in court, where the expert witness is often the key element. This should also be the case in statutory law and regulation. Unfortunately this seems to be the exception rather than the rule, at least in the recent past. The development of technical legislation must be influenced by the state of science. Similarly, the development of regulations based on technical legislation must be done within a scientific framework. And once regulations are in place, there should be periodic scientific reviews to allow for the changes that inevitably occur in any science-based area.

I do not imply that science should be divorced from such regulatory activities as standard setting, enforcement, and so on. I do say that the process of scientific definition and that of regulatory decision should not be in the same hands. A failure to recognize the differences between—and the essential separateness of—scientific definition and legal decision has led to our present direction—or, I should say, misdirection—in environmental legislation and regulation. We have been duped into believing that health and environmental problems have only political solutions, when in fact meaningful solutions will come only if we apply science and technology before we make social and legal decisions.

For the past ten years we have been building at various government levels a large body of environmental legislation and regulation. Most of these rules have been developed in response to social pressures of one kind or another, and these social forces have usually been narrowly focused. Public interest organizations have often been the prime movers for environmental laws and regulations. In response to these pressures, legislative bodies write laws that seem to be beneficial. But the administration of these laws is turned over to agencies that may or may not interpret the basic intentions of the laws in the same way as the legislatures did. Faced with this situation, the laws are commonly rewritten in the courts when one side or the other seeks judicial relief or support.

All this can take years to be worked out, and in the meantime no one benefits. Requiring optimum scientific definition before making regulatory decisions does consume up-front time, but such a practice also prevents ill-considered regulatory litigation and thus accelerates the nation's environmental protection efforts.

The climate in which environmental laws are written and environmental regulations promulgated is currently difficult. Legislators and regulators are subject to many different pressures—from public interest groups, industries, the media, the economy, even other regulatory agencies with competing objectives. Environmental agencies are often asked to do far more than they can realistically be expected to do with too few scientific tools and in too short a time. Information in the environmental area ranges from the tragically inaccurate to the esoterically scientific. Somewhere in the welter of myth, fear, suspicion, theory, and fact lies the information that is needed.

The best way I know to properly separate science from the regulatory process—as well as to provide for the adequacy of science in the legislative and regulatory structure—is to establish a science panel. This is not a new idea. The American Industrial Health Council (AIHC) has been working on the idea for more than four years. An AIHC proposal has undergone a peer review by eminent scientists and also has been reviewed by a number of professional societies, which, by and large, support it. Some regulatory agencies have opposed the concept because they see a science panel as a threat. But I believe the opposite is true because such a panel would neither change an agency's need for its own scientific expertise nor impinge in any way on the agency's regulatory authority. Rather it would give the agencies access to a wider body of scientific knowledge than they can now easily acquire.

A science panel would perform risk estimations on a case-by-case basis for the benefit of all federal regulatory agencies. The agencies would then make regulatory decisions based on the assessments of the science panel. It would be the job of the science panel, for example, to determine whether a material is likely to cause cancer or to induce other adverse chronic health effects. Such determinations involve scientific rather than regulatory judgments, and they should be made by a centrally located panel of eminent scientists separate from the regulatory agencies whose actions would be affected by scientific determinations.

The value of an eminent science panel cannot be doubted: witness, for example, Governor Hugh A. Carey's appointment of Dr. Lewis Thomas to head a panel to find out the facts about Love Canal, New York.

Three results can be expected if industry and the federal government work together consistently through a science panel:

—our workplaces and products will not contain unreasonable risks;

—there will be consistency in regulatory decisions and actions, which may in time lead to credibility among media and public interest groups;

—there will be an opportunity for industry to earn public credibility and continue to stay in business.

Workshop Participants

with their affiliations at the time of the workshop

Paulette Altringer *Science Adviser to Congressman Don Ritter*

Edwin L. Behrens *Procter and Gamble Manufacturing Company*

Charles Benbrook *House Committee on Agriculture*

Jackson Browning *Union Carbide Corporation*

Robert W. Crandall *Brookings Institution*

J. Clarence Davies *Conservation Foundation*

Joanne Glisson *Senate Committee on Labor and Human Resources*

Leonard Guarria *American Industrial Health Council*

John E. Kelsey *Burroughs Wellcome Company*

Lester B. Lave *Carnegie Mellon University*

William McCarville *Monsanto Company*

John Morrall *Office of Management and Budget*

Robert Nicholas *House Committee on Science and Technology*

Sandra Panem *Brookings Institution*

Rustum Roy *Brookings Institution*

Robert Smerko *American Chemical Society*

Bruce L. R. Smith *Brookings Institution*

Barbara Souder *Committee on Labor and Human Resources*

Donald Stevenson *Shell Development Company*

Gary A. Strobel *Occupational Safety and Health Administration*